Writing Flow

Chad Billiris

TO THE TEACHER

Writing is a difficult skill to master in a student's first language and all the more challenging in a second language. While students often find it difficult to organize their thoughts and ideas on paper, it seems that the process of acclimating themselves with the standards and process of academic writing is often most demanding. Writing Flow, however, is designed to address and fix these exact problems. With the help of this book, teachers can help their students not only organize their ideas better, but also begin to familiarize themselves with the standards and process of academic writing.

Who can benefit from this book?

While it is my belief that students of all ages and levels can benefit from this book, it is specifically designed for low-intermediate college and university students. It is intended for students who are learning English writing for both academic and business purposes.

How is Writing Flow organized?

Writing Flow is divided into twelve units, each designed to teach the students a different writing skill, grammatical aspect, as well as new vocabulary. Based on a process writing approach, the first seven units (excluding unit 5, a review unit) are designed to help students becoming acclimated with the standards and process of academic writing in a gradual step-by-step progression.

- Unit 1: Basic sentence construction and punctuation
- Unit 2: Pre-writing and brainstorming
- Unit 3: Topic sentence
- Unit 4: Supporting and concluding sentences
- Unit 6: Introductory paragraphs
- Unit 7: Concluding paragraphs

The remaining units, 8 through 12, (except for unit 9, a review unit) are designed to branch out and introduce students to forms of writing other than those in the academic classroom.

- Unit 8: Movie reviews
- Unit 10: Giving instructions on how to make something

- Unit 11: Cover letters and resumes
- Unit 12: Business letters and envelope writing

Each unit ends with a structured writing assignment that provides an opportunity for students to use everything which was presented in the unit. In addition, at the end of each unit, students are encouraged to not only double check their own work, but to also help proofread a partners', in order to facilitating writing skills.

How should I progress through each lesson?

Teachers are encouraged to adapt this book to their current teaching context, considering their current students' levels, as well as time alloted per class each week. Time and level permitting, I would recommend teaching ***Writing Flow*** in a page-by-page manner, starting with "To the Student" and continuing until unit 12. Below I illustrate a suggested thirteen step tutorial for teaching each unit:

First:

To start a lesson, have the students first look over the ***In this unit you will learn how to section.*** For this section, it is not important for the teacher to go in depth about each topic. Simply explain to the students that these things are considered important in this unit.

Second:

Have students read the example composition. Each unit provides an example composition at both the beginning and the end of each unit. Each example composition is designed to give students a standard point of reference from which to work. By reading each example composition, students should gain an understanding of the quality of work that is expected of them, as well as tools from which they can begin to create their own compositions. Teachers should draw students' attention to unfamiliar words and phrases. In addition, teachers should help students recognize the overall theme of the chapter which they are currently studying. Next, teachers should explain the type of assignment that will be required of the students at the end of the unit, followed by a brief warm-up discussion based on the questions provided. Often times students can express themselves verbally better than they can in written form. Having students first discuss the topic at hand orally before writing can help students organize their ideas more logically to create better writing compositions later.

Third:

Teachers should move lesson–by–lesson through the unit, continually drawing students' attention to how each lesson will later relate to their writing assignment. While each individual lesson teaches something different, it should be understood by the teacher, and the student, that in the end every lesson has the same purpose of making the student's final composition as strong and polished as possible. It should also be noted that teachers are encouraged to have students exchange their work or even at times have them rewrite questions from the book on the board. By doing such activities as these, students should be encouraged to develop their own hypothesis about writing, as well as learn from others' mistakes and successes.

Fourth:

Once all lessons are coved in a single unit, the teacher should have the students read over the final example in the same manner as was conducted in the introductory example.

Fifth:

Once students have firmly digested the last example, the teacher should assign the unit's composition assignment, explicitly explaining each grading criteria in relation to what was covered in the present unit. This should be followed by a thorough explanation of the assignment layout.

Sixth:

It is at step six that the teacher should take a step back, allowing the students to discover and learn a bit on their own. It is okay to answer students' questions, however, try and encourage them to use examples from the chapter and their own knowledge to help answer their own questions.

Seventh:

After each student has finished their composition, encourage them to use the ***Self Check–List*** to help revise their own work.

Eighth:

When students feel that they have satisfactorily finished the assignment to the best of their ability, they can then pass their composition to a partner. Each partner should take their job as editor seriously, using the ***Peer Review Sheet*** as a guide to help them edit their partner's paper.

Ninth:

Once each student has reviewed and edited their partner's paper, they should pass it back and discuss both the good points and bad points that they observed in their partner's work. It is at this point that the original author of the composition can respond and clarify anything that may not have understood, before revising their paper one last time.

Tenth:

At this step, students should revise their assignments one last time, based on the corrections given to them from their partner, before submitting it to the teacher.

Eleventh:

It is here that the teacher should carefully check and evaluate their student's assignments, providing helpful comments and feedback, to facilitate step twelve.

Twelfth:

Teachers should pass back the students' compositions and answer any questions that students might have. In addition, the teacher should diagram on the board one or two common errors that seemed to be consistent throughout the majority of the assignments.

Thirteenth:

Last, teachers should have the students rewrite their assignments before turning them back in again for final grading.

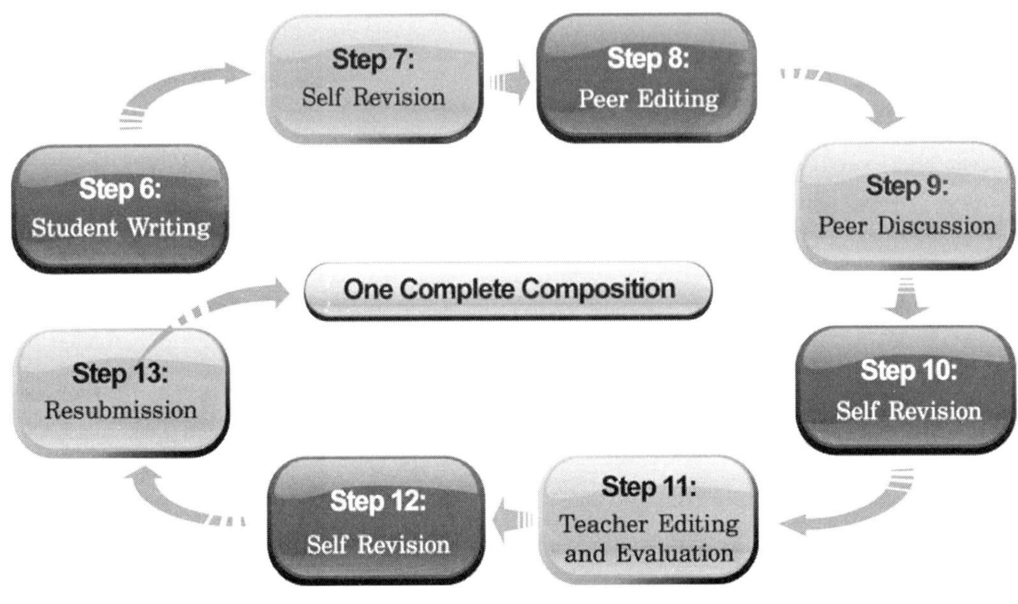

TO THE STUDENT

Writing is a very important part of academics, and while not easy, with consistent effort and focus, you can become an excellent writer. The purpose of Writing Flow is to help you recognize and produce the sort of writing that will be expected of you in academic situations.

During this course, you will be asked to produce a variety of composition assignments. Each assignment will be explained thoroughly and you will be given ample opportunities to ask questions. Please don't be afraid to take risks and ask for clarification on topics of uncertainty. Understand that we as a class are taking on the challenge of writing together and everybody has something worthy of contribution.

In this course I encourage you to:

- work as hard as you can in every class
- ask as many questions as possible
- don't be shy or embarrassed by your mistakes
- treat your partner's work as if it were your own
- come to every class prepared
- write as much as possible, in and out of class

Every class you will need:

- your book
- a pencil and eraser
- a dictionary and thesaurus
- a notebook to be used for in-class writing

CONTENTS

Writing Flow

Unit 01 Basics

▶ **In this unit, you will learn how to ...**

- identify subjects and predicates
- identify and use simple subjects and simple predicates
- identify the use of a period, question mark, and an exclamation mark
- identify and correct sentence fragments
- identify and correct run-on sentences
- expand your vocabulary when writing

1. Read the sentences below then discuss the meanings of any unfamiliar words or phrases. Pay special attention to the bold-faced words. Discuss your hobby with your partner.

My Hobby

1. My hobby is playing basketball.
2. I play basketball everyday.
3. I am **a member of** my university basketball club.
4. I am good at shooting.
5. I am not good at **dribbling.**

At the end of this unit, you will be asked to write five complete sentences about your hobby.

LESSON 1 WHAT MAKES A SENTENCE?

What is a sentence?

A sentence ***is traditionally defined as a group of words that expresses a complete thought.*** The thought a sentence expresses involves a grammatical relationship between a ***subject*** (S) and a ***predicate*** (P).

Example: The rain fell heavily through the night
(S: The rain; P: fell heavily through the night)

The ***subject*** of a sentence is always a noun, a pronoun, a verb, or a clause that functiond like a noun or pronoun. Simply put, the ***subject*** of a sentence is the "thing" which is doing something.

The ***predicate*** of a sentence always contains a verb. The ***predicate*** can, however, include other words, such as prepositions, adjectives, adverbs, nouns, and pronouns. Simply put, the ***predicate*** of a sentence describes the action of the subject.

The ***simple subject*** of a sentence is the single noun or pronoun that is its central subject. An exception to this would include multiword proper nouns such as ***Seoul Tower***.

The ***simple predicate*** of a sentence is the central verb in a sentence. Simply put, the verb which describes the action of the simple subject.

1. Identify the subject and predicate in each sentence below.

a. Spiders have eight legs.

b. The American Civil War lasted from 1861 to 1865.

c. Many real estate agents predict housing prices will continue to fall.

d. Many students reacted unhappily to the increase in homework.

e. Cats meow.

LESSON 2 SIMPLE SUBJECTS & SIMPLE PREDICATES

Simple subject:

The simple subject of a sentence is the main single noun or pronoun in the sentence.

SS SP

ex. J.K. Rowling wrote *Harry Potter and the Sorcerer's Stone* in 1997.

Simple predicate:

The simple predicate of a sentence is its verb.

1. Identify the simple subject and simple predicate in each sentence. Underline the simple subject and circle the simple predicate.

a. Busy rabbits hopped in the grass.

b. The people screamed loudly outside the building.

c. A box of chocolates arrived from Steven.

d. The woman in the red shirt is my aunt.

e. The children drew pictures in class today.

f. The car across the street has a flat tire.

LESSON 3 USING SIMPLE SUBJECTS

1. Choose one of the following simple subjects to complete each sentence below.

athletes	doctor
Dentists	bikes
Scuba divers	rafts
music	Snowboarders

a. A ____________________ is a person who helps sick people.

b. ____________________ fix and clean people's teeth.

c. White-water ____________________ must be made of tough material.

d. ____________________ sometimes choose to swim with dangerous sharks.

e. Mountain ____________________ must be strongly made for riding over rough roads.

f. ____________________ use special bindings to keep their feet from slipping off the board.

h. Loud ____________________ can cause hearing loss.

i. Well-trained ____________________ must workout constantly to keep in shape.

LESSON 4 WRITING SIMPLE SUBJECTS IN SENTENCES

1. Use each of these words as the simple subject in a sentence.

   a. teacher

   ____

   b. cell-phone

   ____

   c. Peter

   ____

   d. mother

   ____

Unit 01

LESSON 5 USING SIMPLE PREDICATES

1. Choose one of the following simple predicates, or verbs, to complete each sentence below.

live	sip	eat
roam	dance	grow
float	study	
build	contain	

a. Women in beautiful dresses ____________________ around the room.

b. You can ____________________ juice from a straw.

c. Several kinds of boats ____________________ in the ocean.

d. Deer, wolves, and other animals ____________________ through the forest.

e. My friends like to ____________________ chicken and pizza.

f. Birds ____________________ in huge nests in tree branches.

g. Different nuts and fruits ____________________ on many trees.

h. Some children's toys ____________________ dangerous chemicals.

i. Students ____________________ many subjects in school.

j. We can ____________________ a campfire with this scrap wood.

LESSON 6 USING SIMPLE PREDICATES IN A SENTENCE

1. Use each word below as the simple predicate in a sentence.

a. jump

____

b. make

____

c. teach

____

d. buy

____

LESSON 7 PUNCTUATION

All complete sentences must end with one of three punctuation marks: a period, a question mark, or an exclamation mark.

Periods are used to end a statement.
e.x. I am a student.

Question marks are used to end a question.
e.x. What is your favorite color?

Exclamation marks are used to end a sentence of extreme feeling.
e.x. My house is on fire!

1. Use the correct punctuation mark to end each sentence below.

a. I like chocolate ice-cream and cake

b. That man just stole my purse

c. Where is the best place to catch a taxi to Gangnam Station

e. How old is that temple over there

f. We met three years ago on a bus to Busan

2. Make your own sentence to match the punctuation mark given.

a. (period)

____

b. (question mark)

____

c. (exclamation mark)

____

LESSON 8 SENTENCE FRAGMENTS

What is a sentence fragment?

Fragments are sentences that are missing either a subject or a predicate, or don't express a complete thought.

ex. Went to a movie.(fragment) *We* went to a movie. (Correct)

Because it was hot.(fragment) I opened the door because it was hot. (Correct)

1. Try to turn each fragment below into a grammatically correct sentence. There may be more than one possible correct answer.

a. went home

____

b. After he got home

____

c. bought a pizza

____

d. a lot of fun

____

LESSON 9 "RUN–ON" SENTENCES

What is a "run-on" sentence?

Run–on sentences are single sentences that should be divided into two or more smaller sentences.

ex. The man wore a big, blue shirt, it was too big. (Run–on)
The man wore a big, blue shirt. It was too big. (Correct)

1. Rewrite each run-on sentence.

a. I ate a hot–dog, a hamburger, a slice of pizza, and an apple, everything was delicious.

____

____

b. Yesterday, I went to a baseball game with my friends in the afternoon, then at night we went to a bar for some drinks.

____

____

c. I live in Seoul it is the capital of South Korea.

____

LESSON 10 EXAMPLE

My Hobby

1. My hobby is playing the piano.
2. My piano was made in Italy.
3. I love to play Beethoven's music.
4. I am the only person in my family who can play the piano.
5. I want to be a professional pianist someday.

Assignment

1. Using the example from page 11, write 5 grammatically correct sentences about your hobby. All spelling mistakes will result in an automatic 5 point deduction from your grade. You will be graded as follows:

Followed the correct layout	/ 5
Wrote about your hobby	/ 5
Wrote five grammatically correct sentences	/ 5
Ended each sentence with the correct punctuation	/ 5
Total score:	/ 20

Assignment Layout

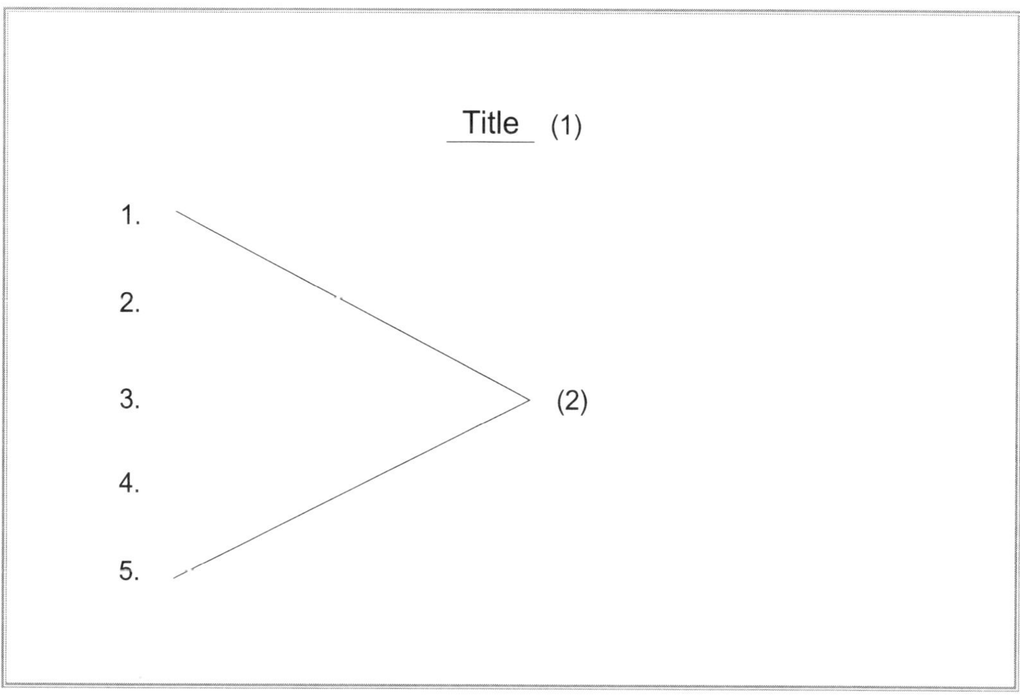

1. The title of your assignment will be "My Hobby". The title should be placed in the center of your page and underlined. The title should be slightly larger than your other writing.

2. Each sentence should be numbered and begin on the left hand side of the page. There should be two spaces between each sentence.

Self Check-List

1. Use the check-list below to make sure you have completed the assignment correctly.

Did you...	Yes	No
follow the correct layout?		
write about your hobby?		
make five grammatically correct sentences?		
end each sentence with the correct punctuation?		

Peer Review

1. Draw a circle around all of the simple subjects in your partner's sentences.
2. Draw a triangle around all of the simple predicates in your partner's sentences.
3. Do all of your partner's sentences talk about the same hobby?
   If not, write the off topic sentences below.

   ____

   ____

5. What is your partner's best sentence? Please write it below.

   ____

4. Use the check-list below to make sure your partner has completed the assignment correctly.

Did your partner...	Yes	No
follow the correct layout?		
write about their hobby?		
make five grammatically correct sentences?		
end each sentence with the correct punctuation?		

5. Discuss your findings and results with your partner.

Unit 02 Who am I?

▶ **In this unit, you will learn how to ...**

- use an **idea web** to help organize your thoughts before writing
- make sentences using **be verbs**
- make sentences using **like + an infinitive**
- connect sentences with **and** & **but**
- organize an e-mail letter with a greeting and a closing
- expand your vocabulary

1. Read the letter below then discuss the meanings of any unfamiliar words or phrases. Pay special attention to the bold-faced words in the letter. Discuss your hobby with your partner.

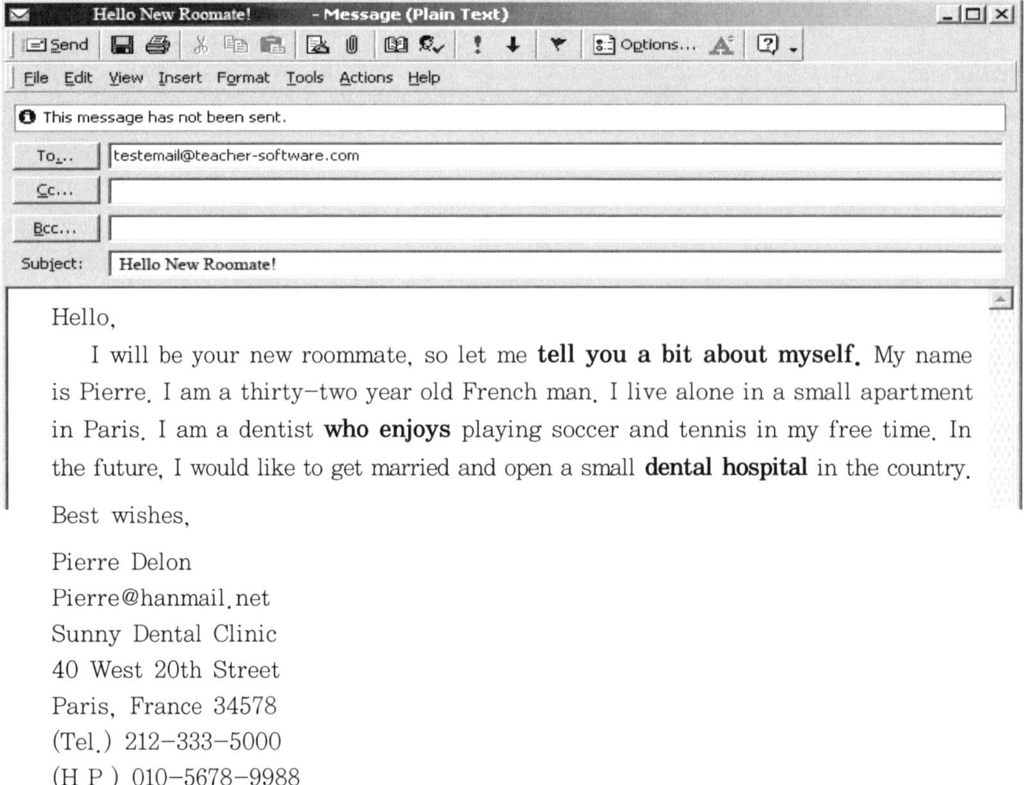

Hello,

I will be your new roommate, so let me **tell you a bit about myself.** My name is Pierre. I am a thirty-two year old French man. I live alone in a small apartment in Paris. I am a dentist **who enjoys** playing soccer and tennis in my free time. In the future, I would like to get married and open a small **dental hospital** in the country.

Best wishes,

Pierre Delon
Pierre@hanmail.net
Sunny Dental Clinic
40 West 20th Street
Paris, France 34578
(Tel.) 212-333-5000
(H.P.) 010-5678-9988

At the end of this unit, you will be asked to write a self-introductory e-mail to a fictitious roommate.

LESSON 1 WRITING FOCUS: PRE-WRITING AND BRAINSTORMING

Before writing you should always organize your thoughts first. A good way to do this is by making an ***Idea web.*** In an ***Idea web*** you can write words, phrases, or sentences.

words → French, athletic
phrases → from Paris, like wine
sentences → I'm 32 years old. I live alone.

1. Pierre's ***Idea Web*** using the topic "Who am I?"

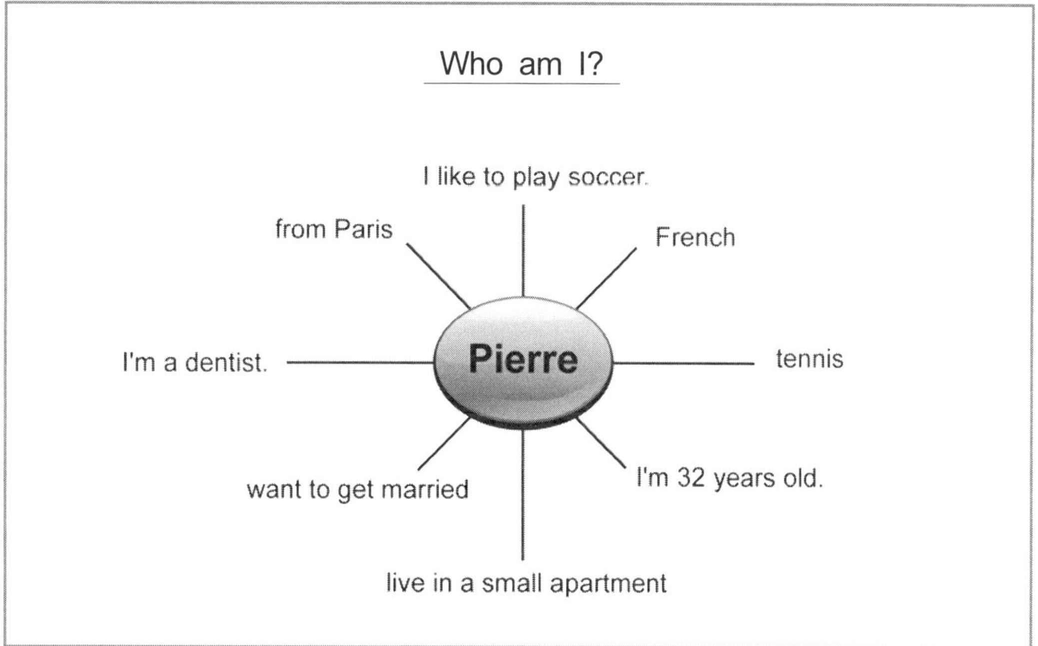

2. Read Pierre's ***Idea Web*** one more time. Put a triangle around the words, a rectangle around the phrases, and a circle around the sentences Pierre wrote.

3. Now brainstorm the topic "**Who am I?**" Write your name in the circle. Then write as many words, phrases, and sentences as you can about yourself.

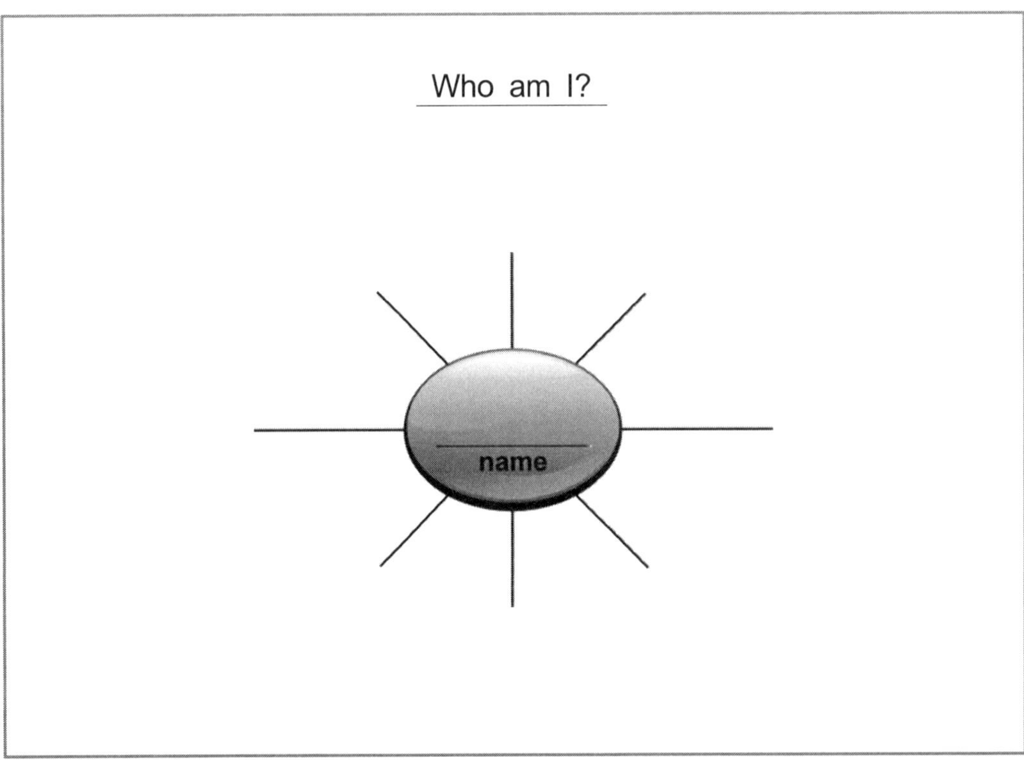

4. Now look at your ***Idea Web*** one more time. Try to think about 3 things from your *idea web* that you most want other people to know about you. Once you have decided what you want then to know about you, write the ideas in sentence form on the lines below. Rank the sentences from the most to least important.

1. ______________________________

2. ______________________________

3. ______________________________

LESSON 2 LANGUAGE FOCUS: USING "BE" VERBS

Subject +Be Verb + (Article) + (Adjective) +Noun

Subject	Be Verb	Article	Adjective	Noun
I	am	a/an	pretty	student
You		a/an	smart	teacher
We	are	X	strong	men
They		X	short	trees
He		a/an	cute	boy
She	is	a/an	outgoing	girl
It		a/an	old	dog

Note For things we own, including our hair color, we use the word *have*.

I have black hair. We have a dog.

1. Use a *Be* Verb and an adjective to complete each sentence below.

a. I am a boy. → I _____ a ___________ boy.

b. We are a family. → We ___________ a _____________ family.

c. They are shoes. → They ___________ _________ shoes.

d. It is a cat. → It ____ a ____________ cat.

e. You are a student. → You _________ a ___________ student.

LESSON 3 LANGUAGE FOCUS: LIKE + INFINITIVE

Subject +Verb + Infinitive +Noun

Subject	Verb	Infinitive	Noun
I	like	to play	tennis.
You		to drink	beer.
He	likes	to eat	pizza.
She		to watch	movies.
John (name)		to sing	ballads.
They	like	to draw	pictures.
We		to read	novels.

Note To make a question simply place the words "do" or "does" at the beginning of each sentence.

1. Use the words or word(s) in the brackets below to answer each question with a full sentence.

   a. What do you like to do on the weekends?

   ______________________________ (go fishing)

   b. What does she like to eat?

   ______________________________ (chicken)

2. Ask your partner each question and write their answer on the lines below.

   a. What do you like to do on Saturday night?

   ____

   b. What do you like to do with your family?

   ____

LESSON 4 LANGUAGE FOCUS: CONNECTING SENTENCES

You can use ***and*** or ***but*** to connect two sentences. A comma ***(,)*** should be placed before **and** or **but** in a sentence. Look at the examples below.

Use the word ***and*** to connect two sentences with similar information.

I am Canadian. I live in Toronto.
I am Canadian, and I live in Toronto.

Use the word ***but*** to connect two sentences of contrasting information.

I am Canadian. I live in South Korea.
I am Canadian, but I live in South Korea.

1. Use the words "and" or "but" to connect the sentences below.

a. I like pizza. I like donuts.

____

b. I have traveled to Japan. I have traveled to Spain.

____

c. I am Chinese. I cannot speak Chinese.

____

d. I live in Seoul. I don't like cities.

____

LESSON 5 ANALYZING SENTENCES: A LITTLE ABOUT PIERRE

(1) My name is Pierre. (2) I am a thirty–two year old French man. (3) I live alone in a small apartment in Paris. (4) I am a dentist who enjoys playing soccer and tennis in my free time. (5) In the future, I would like to get married and open a small dental clinic in the country.

1. Using Pierre's example above write similar sentences below with the words given.

HINT >> You may have to rearrange the words in the sentence.

a. My / Sally (sentence 1)

____

b. I am German / 40 years old (sentence 2)

____

c. mother, father, younger brother/ apartment in Jamsil (sentence 3)

____

d. secretary / watching movies (sentence 4)

____

e. Someday / buy my own apartment (sentence 5)

____

LESSON 6 ORGANIZATION FOCUS: GREETINGS AND CLOSINGS

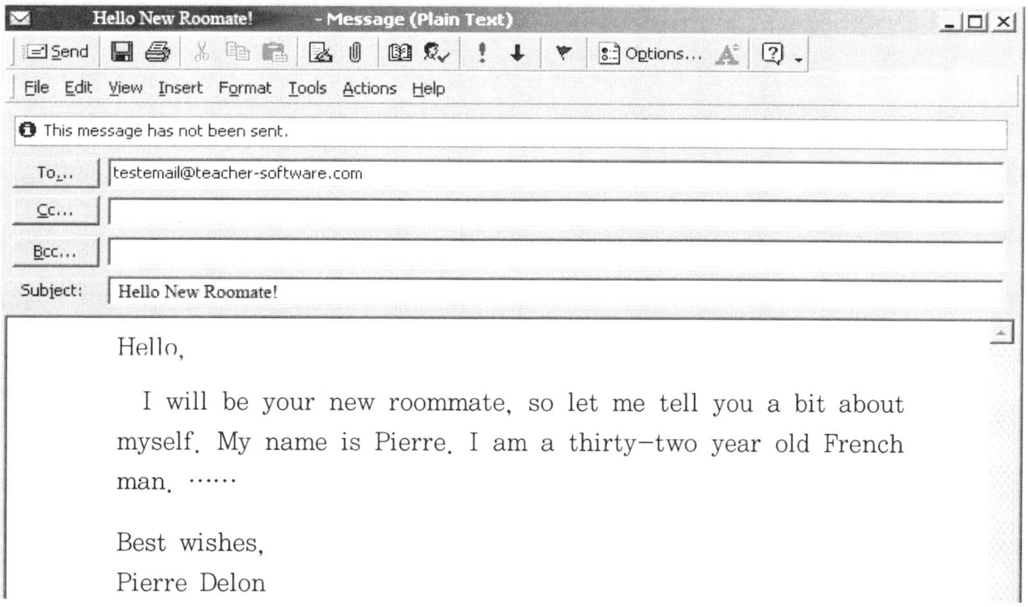

Hello New Roomate! - Message (Plain Text)

Send | Options...

File Edit View Insert Format Tools Actions Help

This message has not been sent.

To... testemail@teacher-software.com

Cc...

Bcc...

Subject: Hello New Roomate!

Hello,

I will be your new roommate, so let me tell you a bit about myself. My name is Pierre. I am a thirty-two year old French man. ……

Best wishes,
Pierre Delon

1. Read Pierre's e-mail letter of introduction. Then write a similar letter of introduction about yourself. Be sure to include a greeting, body, and a closing.

____
(greeting)

____

____
(body)

____
(closing)

____
(your name)

Greetings	Closings
Dear____________, Hello! Hi there,	Sincerely, Yours truly, Best wishes, Until next time,

LESSON 7 ORGANIZATION FOCUS: PARTS OF AN E-MAIL LETTER

1. Read Pierre's e-mail letter of introduction. Follow the instructions below.

Hello,

I will be your new roommate, so let me tell you a bit about myself. My name is Pierre. I am a thirty-two year old French man. I live alone in a small apartment in Paris. I am a dentist who enjoys playing soccer and tennis in my free time. In the future, I would like to get married and open a small dental hospital in the country.

Best wishes,
Pierre Delon
Pierre@hanmail.net
Sunny Dental Clinic
40 West 20th Street
Paris, France 34578
(Tel.) 212-333-5000
(H.P.) 010-5678-9988

a. Circle the greeting.

b. Draw a rectangle around the body.

c. Draw a triangle around the closing.

2. Below is an example of a basic e-mail signature. Look at the example and write your own.

E-mail signature	Your E-mail signature
Pierre Delon *Pierre@hanmail.net* Sunny Dental Clinic 40 West 20th Street Paris, France 34578 (Tel.) 212-333-5000 (H.P.) 010-5678-9988	

LESSON 8 VOCABULARY FOCUS

1. Examine the use of each word or phrase underlined below and see if you can guess the meaning. If you are not sure of the meaning, ask a classmate, or check your dictionary. Once you have found the meanings of all the words and phrases, create your own sentences with the bold-faced words and phrases.

   a. I am ***studying to be*** a doctor.

   b. ***In my free-time*** I like to play computer games.

   c. I am an ***enthusiastic*** snowboarder.

   d. I am an ***aspiring*** writer.

   e. I am an ***experienced*** mountain climber.

   f. I have always been jealous of my friends who have several ***siblings***.

   g. My father ***passed away*** when I was young.

   h. I am ***well-acquainted*** with western culture.

   i. You should know that I am a ***neat freak***.

a. ______________________________

b. ______________________________

c. ______________________________

d. ______________________________

e. ______________________________

f. ______________________________

g. ______________________________

h. ______________________________

i. ______________________________

LESSON 9 EXAMPLE LETTER

Dear Mr. and Mrs. Smith,

I will be your homestay guest for this year, so let me tell you a little about myself. My name is Miniko Hiroshima. I am a 23 year old Japanese woman. I am currently studying to become a lawyer at Tokyo University. One day I hope to have my own law firm in Japan. I live with my mother and father in Oshima, Tokyo. I have traveled a lot, but I have never been to Canada. I love sports, and exercising. In my free time, I like listening to music, especially ballads. Do you like ballads? What are your interests? Please write back and tell me about yourself.

Yours truly,
Minika Hiroshima
mk2@yahoo.com
32 East 15 street
Oshima, Tokyo 68742
(Tel.) 212-333-8000
(H.P.) 016-478-1947

Assignment

Using the example from page 26, you have to write a one paragraph letter introducing yourself to your new fictitious Australian university roommate. You will be graded according to the chart below. All spelling mistakes will result in an automatic 5 point deduction from your grade.

Followed the correct layout	/5
Had a greeting, and a closing that included a signature	/5
Had at least 3 sentences connected with ***and*** or ***but***	/5
Wrote about your name, age, nationality, and gender	/5
Wrote about your likes and dislikes	/5
Asked at least two different questions	/5
Total Score	/30

Assignment Layout

Greeting, (1)

   XXXXXXXXXXXXXXXXXXXXXXXXXXX
XXXXXXXXXXXXXXXXXXXXXXXXXXXXX
XXXXXXXXXXXXXXXXXXXXXXXXXXXXX

Body (2)

Closing, (3)
Signature (4)

1. Your greeting should be in the top left corner of your page. It should begin on the far left edge of your page and end with a comma.

2. The first sentence in your body should be indented. The remaining sentences in your body should align with your greeting. Additionally, all of your sentences should align on the right side of your page evenly. There should be two spaces between each line.

3. Your closing should align with both your greeting and your body. Your closing, similar to your greeting, should also be followed by a comma.

4. Your signature should come after your closing and does not need a comma. First, write your email address. Second, write your home address *in this order*; your street, town, city, country, and zip code. Third, write your home telephone number. Last, write your cell-phone/ hand-phone number.

Self Check-List

1. Use the check-list below to make sure you have completed the assignment correctly.

Did you...	Yes	No
follow the correct layout?		
write a greeting, and a closing that included a signature?		
write at least 3 sentences using ***and*** or ***but*** ?		
write about your name, age, nationality, and gender?		
write about your likes and dislikes?		
ask at least two different questions?		
make any spelling mistakes?		

Peer Review

1. Read your partner's assignment. Do you feel that your partner introduced themselves well? Please explain why or why not.

2. What sentence did you find most interesting? Please write it below.

3. Did you find any incorrect sentences or spelling mistakes? If so please write them below.

4. Use the check-list below to make sure you partner has completed the assignment correctly.

Did your partner...	Yes	No
follow the correct layout?		
write a greeting, and a closing that included a signature?		
write at least 3 sentences using ***and*** or ***but*** ?		
write about their name, age, nationality, and gender?		
write about their likes and dislikes?		
ask at least two different questions?		
make any spelling mistakes?		

5. Discuss your findings and results with your partner.

Writing Flow

Unit 03 All About My Friend

▶ **In this unit, you will learn how to ...**

- use adjectives to describe personalities and appearances
- gather common ideas in an idea web
- write a topic sentence
- use pronouns and possessive adjectives
- use ***as a result***, ***Therefore***, and ***consequently*** to show an effect
- expand your vocabulary when writing

1. Read the essay below and then discuss the meanings of any unfamiliar words or phrases. Pay special attention to the bold-faced words and phrases in the composition.
2. Discuss with your partner about whether you know anybody like the person described in this story.

My Friend Jody

My friend Jody is the most ***optimistic person*** that I know, therefore talking to her always cheers me up. ***Just the other day,*** I was ***feeling really down*** about my studies. I had a lot of homework. It was so overwhelming. Consequently, I just wanted to quit school and forget about everything. Suddenly my phone rang. When I answered, it was Jody. I told her about my situation, and asked her what I should do. She told me how doing homework will help me learn important skills, which will later help me ***land a great job***. Her words gave me new energy. As a result, I was able to finish my work. I think that we all should learn to be optimistic like Jody.

Jody's appearance is ***equally as beautiful as her personality***. She has long, wavy, red hair, a slim ***waist line***, and the cutest smile ***anybody as ever seen***. As a result, all of the boys in our school love her, but all of the girls are envious. I once asked her if having so many people envy her made her sad. Answering optimistically, Jody said "no", saying that having people envy her helps her stay in shape and look even better. Consequently, she works out everyday and has a size six waist line. Jody is truly a beautiful girl.

At the end of this unit, you will be asked to write a two paragraph composition about one of your friends. The composition should explain both your friend's personality, as well as their appearance.

Unit 03

LESSON 1 PRE-WRITING AND BRAINSTORMING: PERSONALITY ADJECTIVES

Good Personality Types:

honest	funny	generous	easy-going
ambitious	creative	well organized	patient
trustworthy	optimistic		

Bad Personality Types:

selfish	arrogant	immature	rude
stubborn	pessimistic	aggressive	close-minded
lazy	picky		

1. Try to match the words above with their correct definition below.
   a. Somebody who is very hard to please ____________
   b. Somebody who is not motivated ____________
   c. Somebody who only listens to their own opinions ____________
   d. Somebody who likes to fight with others ____________
   e. Somebody who always thinks the worst ____________
   f. Somebody who never yields to others ____________
   g. Somebody who always thinks positively ____________
   h. Somebody who you can always trust ____________
   i. Somebody who doesn't get angry easily ____________
   j. Somebody who is very neat ____________
   k. Somebody who is good at making things ____________
   l. Somebody who is very hard working ____________
   m. Somebody who has no manners ____________
   n. Somebody who acts like a child ____________
   o. Somebody who likes to boast about themselves ____________
   p. Somebody who is very easy to please ____________
   q. Somebody who is always willing to help others ____________
   r. Somebody who makes you laugh ____________
   s. Somebody who only thinks of themselves ____________
   t. Somebody who always tells the truth ____________

2. With your partner, try to think of some other personality types, which were not listed above.

LESSON 2 PRE-WRITING AND BRAINSTORMING: APPEARANCE ADJECTIVES

1. Look at the pictures below, discuss with your partner how you would describe each person's appearance?

2. Use the vocabulary words from page 32. Think of some of your friends. What kind of personalities do they have? What are some adjectives you would use to describe their appearance? Fill in the chart below.

Friend's Name	Personality	Appearance
Jody	Optimistic	Tall, Beautiful, Long hair

LESSON 3 WRITING FOCUS: GROUPING SIMILAR IDEAS

Once you have made your intial ***idea web*** it is helpful to ***group common ideas***. In addition, ***crossing out ideas that are unrelated*** reduces clutter in your composition later.

1. Look at the ***idea web*** below. The author is going to write a composition explaining their friend's personality.

   a. With your partner, decide why the ideas are grouped together.

   b. With your partner, decide why the two ideas are crossed out.

My Friend Jody

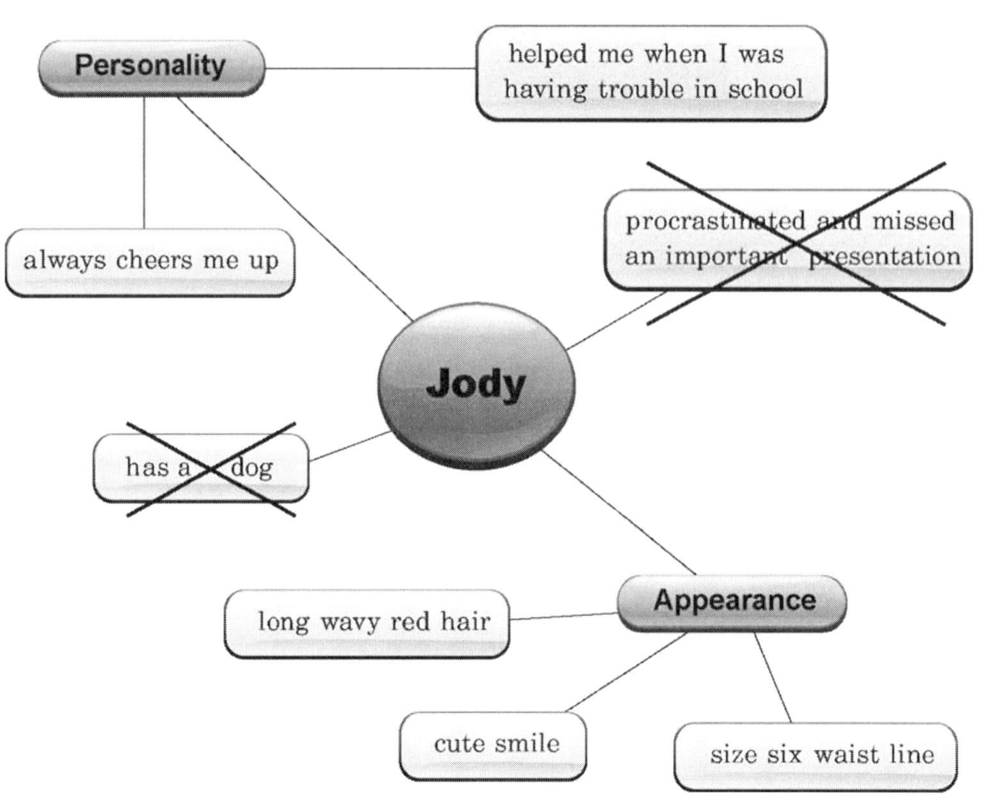

2. Look at the ***idea web*** below. The author is going to write a composition explaining outdoor activities that can be done in South Korea. Decide which items should be grouped together and which items should be crossed out using the example shown on P.34.

Outdoor Activities in South Korea

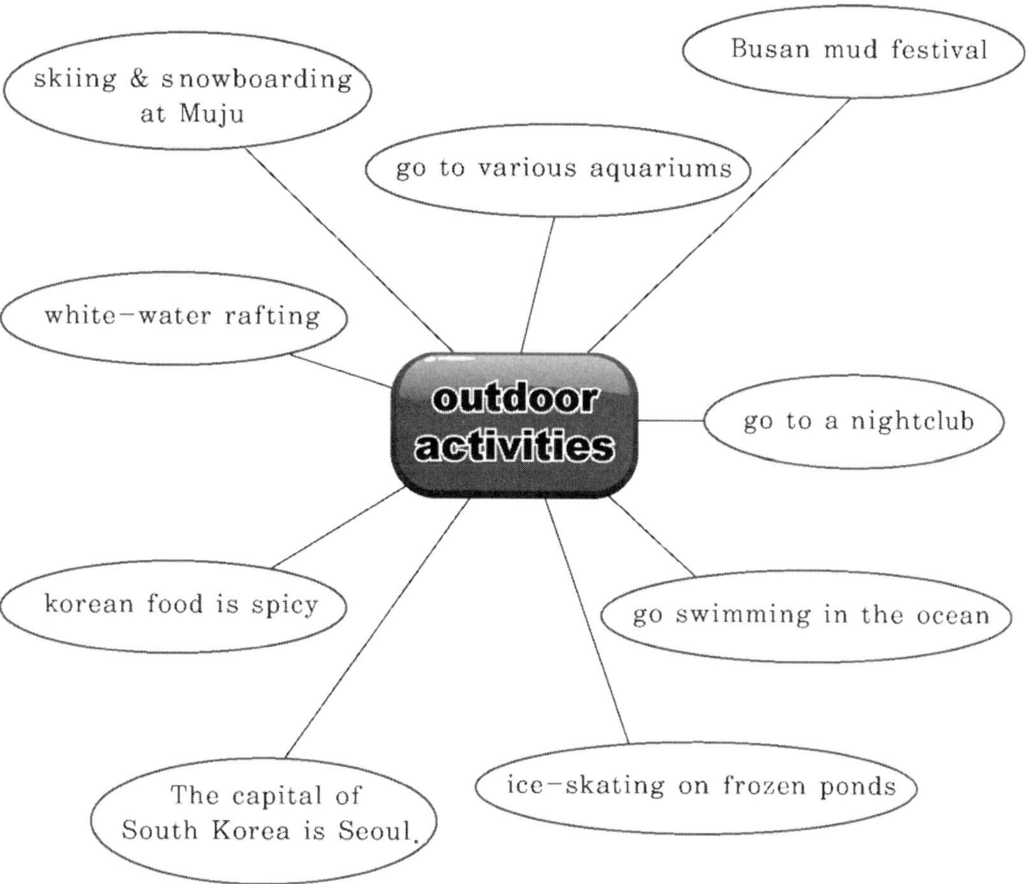

3. Now try to make your own ***idea web*** for a composition explaining one of your friend's personalities. Be sure to group similar ideas. Cross out any unrelated ideas as shown in lesson 3.

LESSON 4 WRITING FOCUS: TOPIC SENTENCES

A topic sentence ***tells the subject of the paragraph and gives a main idea or opinion***. The topic sentence is ***usually*** the ***first*** or ***last*** ***sentence in a paragraph***, but it can be any sentence in the paragraph.

A good ***"strong"*** topic sentence should:

- be one clear thought or idea.
  strong: Kimchi is Korea's most delicious food.
  weak: Korea has a lot of delicious food, and a beautiful culture.
- give the reader an idea about what will be, or has been, presented in the following or previous paragraph.
  strong: Studying English has given me a chance to work abroad.
  weak: I have been studying English for eight years.

A good ***"strong"*** topic sentence should not:

- be too broad.
  weak: Jeju Island is a beautiful place.
  strong: Jeju island has beautiful beaches.
- be too narrow.
  weak: Turtles have a strong shell.
  strong: A turtle's shell is very important for their survival.

1. Circle the topic sentence in each paragraph.

a. Bruce is the most athletic person I know. Bruce is a member of our high school baseball, football, and basketball team. He was voted best pitcher in our league two years in a row. In addition, he holds our school record for most points scored in a basketball game.

b. Jackie is the kindest person in the world. One day when we were walking home from class we saw an old lady carrying a heavy bag of rice. Jackie asked the lady if she needed help and carried the bag to her house for her. The lady tried to thank him by giving him some money, but Jackie refused it and instead gave her his phone number. He told her to call anytime she needed help.

c. If I need some advice I can always call my mom. My mom is always willing to help me anyway she can. When I am hungry my mom always cooks my favorite foods. I have the best mom in the world.

d. My friend Jack is always eating. He loves fast food, especially hamburgers, and as a result he weighs the most in our class. Since I first met him his waist has gotten bigger and bigger. Consequently, he often can't find pants that fit him. I truly believe that Jack is overweight.

2. Look at the following topic sentence pairs. Choose which topic sentence is better and why. You should be able to explain your choices based on one sentence:
   - not having one clear topic
   - not having stated a main idea or opinion
   - being too narrow
   - being too broad

a. 1. My friend likes baseball.
   2. My friend thinks that baseball is a sport that everybody should play.

b. 1. English is useful.
   2. Fluency in English can help you get a well paying job.

c. 1. Korea has spicy food, as well as sweet food.
   2. Korean food is traditionally very spicy.

d. 1. Apples are red.
   2. Eating an apple a day can improve your health.

e. 1. The last book I read changed my life.
   2. It is good to read a lot of books.

3. Write a good strong topic sentence for each paragraph below.

a. ____. Cell phones should always be carried when going on long trips or when participating in outdoor activities such as mountain climbing. When taking long trips, as well as participating in outdoor activities, there is always a chance of unexpected emergencies arising. In these situations cell phones can often help save lives and protect our friends and family ……

b. ____. At Christmas time it is important to buy presents for family, friends, and co-workers. Failure to buy presents for people can cause them to be upset. This is especially true if they bought you a present, but you forgot or neglected to buy one for them. The problem is that even buying a small present costing no more than ₩10,000 for a few friends or family members will likely coast you a tremendous amount of money. For most people this can cause serious financial problems and even debt ……

c. ____. On average I eat pizza three to four times a week. I love cheese pizza, pepperoni pizza and potato pizza. Any kind of pizza is delicious to me. If I had to choose between eating steak or pizza, I would choose pizza. If I could only eat one food for breakfast, lunch, and dinner everyday of my life, it would be pizza ……

d. ____. Dentists say that you should brush your teeth at lest three times a day. People who don't brush their teeth run the risk of having bad breath and rotten teeth. While some people might feel that a few rotten teeth and a little bad breath is ok, I am sure they won't like the pain of cavities. Not brushing your teeth can cause cavities, causing you extreme pain. This pain can often be so bad that people are unable to eat ……

LESSON 5 LANGUAGE FOCUS: USING PRONOUNS AND POSSESSIVE ADJECTIVES

To avoid repeating names, use pronouns and possessive adjectives.

Subject Pronouns	Object Pronouns	Possessive Adjectives
he She They	him her them	his her their

(Not Good) **Tony** is very ambitious. **Tony** studies for 10 hours a day. **Tony** has the best grades in our class. **Tony's** dream is to become a famous CEO someday.

(Better) **Tony** is very ambitious. **He** studies for 10 hours a day. **He** has the best grades in our class. **His** dream is to become a famous CEO someday.

1. Change the paragraph below by using the correct pronoun or possessive adjective.

a. My friend Scott is the funniest person I know. Therefore, Scott always makes me laugh when I am feeling blue. For example, the other day I failed my math test, even though I studied all night. As a result, I was very upset. Scott saw that I was upset and began telling me jokes. At first, I told Scott to stop, but Scott kept telling joke after joke. Consequently, after a few minutes I was laughing so hard that I thought my stomach was going to explode. As a result, Scott helped me to forget all about my test with his humor, and I was no longer sad anymore.

b. My friend __________ is the funniest person I know. Therefore, ________ always makes me laugh when I am feeling blue. For example, the other day I failed my math test, even though I studied all night. As a result, I was very upset. ________ saw that I was upset and began telling me jokes. At first, I told ________ to stop, but ________ kept telling joke after joke. Consequently, after a few minutes I was laughing so hard that I thought my stomach was going to explode. As a result, ________ helped me to forget all about my test with his humor and I was no longer sad anymore.

LESSON 6 LANGUAGE FOCUS: USING "AS A RESULT" AND "CONSEQUENTLY"

As a result, *therefore,* and *Consequently* all have a similar meaning and are used to connect two ideas. They are used to show that the second sentence was the effect, or result of the first sentence. They can be used at the beginning of a second sentence followed by a comma, or they can join two sentences by proceeding them with a comma followed by ***and*** .

- As a result:

I finally decided to buy a new car. **As a result**, I took a loan out at the bank.
I finally decided to buy a new car, ***and*** **as a result** I took a loan out at the bank.

- Therefore:

My friend wants to be a doctor. **Therefore**, he studies very hard.
My friend wants to be a doctor, ***and*** **therefore** he studies very hard.

- Consequently:

My friend never came to class. **Consequently,** he failed the class.
My friend never came to class, ***and*** **consequently** he failed the class.

1. In section "1" match the sentences from column correctly. Next, in section "2" join each sentence using *As a result*, *therefore,* or *Consequently*

a. I lived in Japan for seven years.
b. My friend doesn't have a car.
c. I cannot see very well.
d. My friend doesn't like animals.

e. I wear glasses.
f. He rides the bus to school
g. I can speak Japanese.
h. She doesn't have any pets.

2.

a. ______________________________

b. ______________________________

c. ______________________________

d. ______________________________

LESSON 7 ANALYZING SENTENCES: SUE IS THE LAZIEST PERSON I KNOW

(1) Sometimes, however, Susan is the laziest person I know. **(2)** As a result, she often misses important deadlines and appointments. **(3)** Last week, for example, she didn't finish a presentation for an important business meeting, because she procrastinated too long. **(4)** Consequently, her boss became very angry and threatened to fire her. **(5)** Being optimistic, however, she didn't let it bother her and instead overslept for work the next day. **(6)** Sue is definitely lazy.

1. Using the example above, write similar sentences belowwith the words given.

a. Kevin / unorganized (sentence 1)

____

b. loses his homework and books. (sentence 2)

____

c. he didn't have his book for grammar class / lost it (sentence 3)

____

d. Teacher / fail him (sentence 4)

____

e. unorganized / didn't bring book next class (sentence 5)

____

f. Kevin / unorganized (sentence 6)

____

LESSON 8 VOCABULARY PRACTICE

1. Examine the use of each word or phrase underlined below and see if you can guess the meaning. If you are not sure of the meaning, ask a classmate or check your dictionary. Once you have found the meanings of all the words and phrases, create your own sentences with the bold-faced words and phrases.

   a. My father likes to **fly off at the handle**.

   b. My sister's room is a **pigsty**.

   c. My friend Dustin is a real **people person**.

   d. My girlfriend always looks **impeccable**.

   e. I like to live a **lavish** lifestyle.

   f. It's important to learn how to **keep your priorities in order**.

   g. My friend Janice always **lives outside of her means**.

   h. I am very **dedicated to** whatever I do.

   i. My friend Jeremy is always **reluctant** to spend money.

   a. ______________________________

   b. ______________________________

   c. ______________________________

   d. ______________________________

   e. ______________________________

   f. ______________________________

   g. ______________________________

   h. ______________________________

   i. ______________________________

LESSON 9 EXAMPLE

My Friend Andrew

Andrew is the kindest person I know. Therefore, he is always willing to help me. One day my car broke down. I didn't know who to call for help, and as a result I called Andrew. He drove out to me right away, and picked me up. In addition, he even recommend a good mechanic to fix my car. Andrew is truly kind.

While many people admire Andrew's kind personality, it's his stunning looks that often impress people most. He is tall, with stylish, short, blonde hair and angel-like blue eyes, and as a result he is one of Korea's top models. As if this were not enough, he also has a great well built body combined with perfect teeth. Consequently, whenever he goes somewhere people always stop and stare. No one can deny that Andrew is very handsome.

Assignment

Using the example from page 44 you have to create a two paragraph story about one of your friend's personalities. You will be graded according to the chart below. In addition, there should be no spelling mistakes. All spelling mistakes will result in an automatic 5 point deduction from your grade.

Followed the correct layout	/5
Had two strong topic sentences	/5
Used pronouns and possessive adjectives	/5
Had a paragraph describing your friend's personality	/5
Had a paragraph describing your friend's appearance	/5
Had at least three sentences connected or starting with ***as a result,*** ***therefore,*** or ***consequently***	/5
Total Score	/30

Assignment Layout

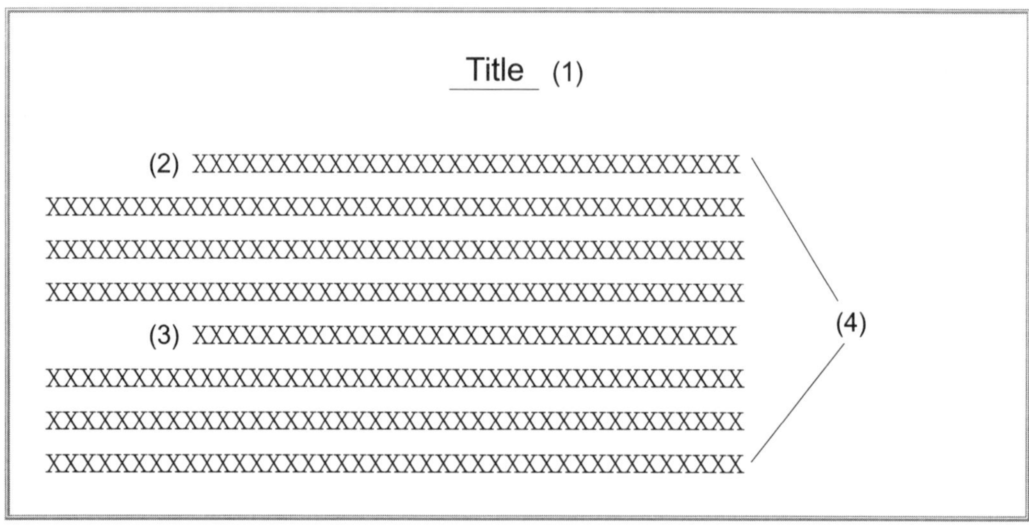

1. Your title should be in the center of your page and underlined. The first letter of your title should be capitalized.

2.-3. The first sentence of each paragraph should be indented.

4. The remaining sentences in your body should align on the right side of your page evenly. There should be two spaces between each line in your composition.

Self Check-List

1. Use the check-list below to make sure you have completed the assignment correctly.

Did you...	Yes	No
follow the correct layout?		
write two strong topic sentences?		
use pronouns and possessive adjectives?		
write a paragraph describing your friend's personality?		
write a paragraph describing your friend's appearance?		
write at least three sentences connected or starting with as a result, therefore, or consequently ?		
make any spelling mistakes?		

Peer Review

1. Read your partner's assignment. Find your partner's topic sentences and write them below. Do you feel these are strong or weak topic sentences and why?

2. Which sentence did you find most interesting? Please write it below.

3. Did you find any incorrect sentences or spelling mistakes? If so, please write them below.

4. Use the check-list below to make sure you partner has completed the assignment correctly.

Did your partner...	Yes	No
follow the correct layout?		
write two strong topic sentences?		
use pronouns and possessive adjectives?		
write a paragraph describing their friend's personality?		
write a paragraph describing their friend's appearance?		
write at least three sentences connected or starting with as a result, therefore, or consequently ?		
make any spelling mistakes?		

5. Discuss your findings and results with your partner.

Writing Flow

Unit 04 My Style!

▶ **In this unit, you will learn how to ...**

- make lists in order to better organize ideas
- write **supporting sentences**
- write **concluding sentences**
- use ***because*** to give a reason
- write **titles**
- expand your vocabulary when writing

1. Read the essay below. Next, discuss the meanings of any unfamiliar words or phrases, including the bold - faced words and phrases in the composition.
2. Ask your partner, what they like better, badminton or rugby?
3. With your partner discuss things you like and dislike.

I Like Badminton More Than Rugby

There are many sports in the world, but there are three reasons why I like playing badminton best. Badminton can be played both indoors and out, and therefore you can always play no matter the weather outside. Badminton is **fast paced** and exciting, as you constantly serve, volley, and smash. Last of all, when you play badminton you don't have to **rely on** teammates because badminton is a one–on–one sport. Badminton really is a cool sport.

My partner Charles, on the other hand, likes playing rugby best. However, I think rugby is too **violent**, and therefore is not good for your body. Another reason I don't like rugby is that you must play it outside, and as a result weather can often affect your **performance**. Finally, I don't like rugby because it is a **team sport**. I only like to play **individual sports**. While Charles may like rugby, I don't.

At the end of this unit, you will be asked to write a two paragraph block style composition about one thing you like and one thing you dislike. The composition should be well written with strong supporting sentences given to support your point of view.

LESSON 1 PRE WRITING AND BRAINSTORMING: MAKING LISTS

1. Try to think of as many words as you can for each category below.

School Subjects	Kinds of Music	Kinds of Movies	Kinds of Food	Kinds of Sports
Math				

2. When writing it can often be helpful to make lists. Lists can help you organize your ideas as well as make connections between two similar or contrasting topics. Similar to idea webs, when making lists you can use words, phrases, or sentences to help organize your thoughts.

Why I like badminton

1. You wear sneakers
2. Hitting the scuttle cock is fun
3. It can be played inside or out
4. All of my friends play badminton
5. Fast paced
6. Badminton is an individual sport.

Why I dislike rugby

1. Violent
2. You wear cleats
3. Played outside
4. It's a team sport
5. It's hard to practice alone
6. There are no ruby fields near my home.

Once you have made two lists try to circle words, phrases, or sentences which you wish to use in your composition.

3. Choose your favorite category from above and select one thing you like and one thing you don't like from it. Using the example above try to make your own lists.

____

a.
b.
c.
d.
e.
f.

____

a.
b.
c.
d.
e.
f.

LESSON 2 WRITING FOCUS: SUPPORTING SENTENCES

Supporting sentences are opinions, examples, or facts, which support or validate your topic sentence.

Topic sentence: Jazz music is excellent for making people feel happy.
Opinion supporting sentence: When people hear the saxophone melody in jazz music it makes people want to smile.

Topic sentence: Jazz music is excellent for making people feel happy.
Example supporting sentence: At the club where I work, whenever they play Jazz music the people always seem very happy.

Topic sentence: Jazz music is excellent for making people feel happy.
Fact supporting sentence: Doctors have found that when people listening to jazz music in the morning it can make them feel happy all day long.

Note While there is no set perfect number of supporting sentences needed to make a paragraph complete, it is commonly felt that the more supporting sentences used, the stronger the paragraph is. Furthermore, the majority of your supporting sentences should be of fact and example. Opinion supporting sentences should be kept to a minimum. For the compositions in this book three to four well written supporting sentences should be sufficient.

1. Read each paragraph below, labeling each supporting sentence as an opinion, example or a fact.

a. In my opinion horror movies should be banned from television. (a) Horror movies have no positive influence on our lives, while they can effect us negatively in various ways. (b) My son once watched a horror movie at his friend's house, and since that time he has not been able to sleep without having nightmares. (c) In addition, the sudden shock of horror movies is also bad for people's hearts. (d) Studies have also revealed that most murderers have reported horror movies as a contributing factor to their violent behavior……

(a) ____________________ (b) ____________________

(c) ____________________ (d) ____________________

b. Soccer is the one sport loved around the world. People's love for soccer can best be seen in the World Cup. (a) Among all international sporting events the World Cup is most watched by people around the world. (b) While some countries don't have a national baseball or an American football team, every country has a national soccer team. (c) Similarly, my school has no sports team other than soccer. (d) Adding to the proof of soccer's popularity, is a recent online survey, in which soccer was voted the world's favorite sport……

(a) ______________________ (b) ______________________

(c) ______________________ (d) ______________________

c. History is the most boring subject in school. (a) Every history class is the same, we just read read read. (b) Because of this history class is much more boring than science class, where we get to move around and use our hands. (c) In history class we never learn about anything related to the world we live in today. (d) In geography class, however, we get to see the world as it is now, which is much more exciting and important for our lives. . .

(a) ______________________ (b) ______________________

(c) ______________________ (d) ______________________

d. I truly believe that night clubs are not good for your health. (a) Night clubs are always filled with cigarette smoke. (b) The smoke is so bad that after you leave your clothes and hair stink like cigarettes. (c) Night clubs are also very noisy. (d) You can barely hear what people are saying and your ears ring for hours after you have left.

(a) ______________________ (b) ______________________

(c) ______________________ (d) ______________________

2. Create your own supporting sentences to match the topic sentence given below.

a. Hamburgers are one of the world's most unhealthy foods.

→ Supporting sentence: ____The fat in hamburgers can clog your arteries, causing a heart attack or even death.

b. Being a university student is more difficult than being a high school student.

→ Supporting sentence: ____________________

____

c. Ballads are very romantic.

→ Supporting sentence: ____________________

____

d. Reading novels in English can help improve your vocabulary.

→ Supporting sentence: ____________________

____

e. Dogs make the best pets.

→ Supporting sentence: ____________________

____

LESSON 3 WRITING FOCUS: CONCLUDING SENTENCES

The concluding sentence in a paragraph, **summaries the authors feelings and thoughts** about the paragraph as a whole. **In many cases it is almost identical to the topic sentence of the paragraph. They may in some cases even be reversible.**

A concluding sentence can:

- restate the topic sentence
- summarize the main idea of a paragraph
- make a prediction concerning the topic of the paragraph
- make a suggestion or give advice regarding the paragraph's topic

A concluding sentence should never:

- state a new thought or idea
- be exactly the same as the topic sentence

1. Circle the concluding sentence in each paragraph.

a. Tomorrow is my birthday. All of my friends are going to come to my house for a party. We are going to sing songs, open presents, and play games. Tomorrow is going to be a wonderful day.

b. Teachers have the best job in the world. Teachers are so lucky because they get to talk all day. At some jobs you can't talk to anybody for hours. That would drive me crazy. Another good thing about being a teacher is that they work inside. Can you imagine having to work outside in August. Being a teacher is a great job.

c. Milk is much healthier for you than juice. Milk contains protein, fat, and vitamins, which the body needs to maintain strength. Juice, on the other hand, is filled with sugar, which makes your body weak. The vitamins in milk can help make your bones and teeth strong, while juice can cause cavities and decreased bone mass. If you want to have a healthy body you should drink milk, not juice.

2. For each paragraph below write your own concluding sentence.

a. Summer is the worst time of the year. The summer heat drains people's energy. It is a fact that people become more lazy in the summer than winter. Due to the increase in temperature in the summer we sweat more. Because of this we have to do laundry more frequently than in the winter.

---

b. Books are better than movies. The first reason that books are better than movies is that they are more portable. You can take a book with you anywhere you go. You cannot, however, take a movie anywhere you go. The second reason that books are better than movies is that they force us to use our imaginations. Many times when we watch a movie we turn our brains off. When reading a book, however, our minds are continually working.

---

c. Kids need physical exercise. Doctors have recently found that children in South Korea are becoming weaker and weaker. Some Doctors believe this is due to lack of physical exercise. In most Korean schools, Math, Science, and English class are considered to be very important. Physical education class, however, is not considered as important.

LESSON 4 LANGUAGE FOCUS: USING "BECAUSE" TO GIVE A REASON

When writing we can use the word **because to explain the reason why we feel a certain way we do.** When "because" joins a main clause and an adverb clause, as in the example below, no comma is needed.

Example:

I like kim chee. I like spicy food.

I like kim chee because I like spicy food.

Incorrect:

I like kim chee. Because I like spicy food.

1. Rewrite the sentences below using because.

a. I want to learn how to cook. I like to eat.

____

b. I am good at basketball. I can jump very high.

____

c. Math is fun. I like to work with numbers.

____

d. English class is very exciting. I like classes were you get to speak a lot.

____

2. Try to make your own sentences joined by because.

a. ______________________________

b. ______________________________

c. ______________________________

d. ______________________________

e. ______________________________

LESSON 5 ORGANIZATION FOCUS: TITLES

Titles are almost always found in the center of the page in academic writing. While titles can be only one word, **titles** should not be too long. Therefore, **titles** exceeding the length of one sentence are considered to be too long. **Titles** should give the reader an idea of what to your composition is about. In addition, all **titles** should be capitalized.

Basic rules for capitalizing titles include:

- Always capitalize the first word of a **title**
- Capitalize every noun, verb, and adverb. This includes all forms of the verb **to be** (be, am, is, are, was, were, been)
- Capitalize prepositions only when
  1. They are five letter long or longer
  2. They are the first or last word of a title
  3. They are part of a phrasal verb (ex. Give Up the Fight)
  4. They are the first word in a compound preposition (ex. Get Off of My Mountain)
- Capitalize each hyphenated word separately according to the rules above

Aesthetic preferences:

- **Titles** can be underlined
- **Titles** can be written in bold-faced

1. Following the rules above to capitalize each title below correctly.

a. lessons of life

____

b. greetings from the grave

____

c. a typical day in my life

____

1. Read each short story below, and decide which title fits best.

a. A man dressed in black stepped on stage and suddenly raised a big black hat into the air. The crowd was very silent. Suddenly the man reached his hand into the hat, and to everybody's surprise, he pulled out a big purple elephant. The man didn't stop there. After the elephant came a lion and a bear. Finally the man took a deep bow and the crowd applauded loudly.

- Red Roses
- A Man and His Hat.
- The Amazing Magician

b. Steve hated school, but he was always the fist student to arrive to class. Steve always sat in the same seat, row two seat number seven. He liked this seat because Nancy always sat in the same eat also, row one seat number six. During class he would often stare at her as she worked, dreaming of someday asking her out.

- A Boy in Love
- Seats in a Classroom
- Nancy's Lucky Day

c. I have tired many vegetables and in my opinion broccoli is the most delicious. Broccoli is filled with vitamins B, A, and C, not to mention it also contains protein, something most vegetables don't. While, broccoli is very nutritious, however, this is not it's most appealing factor. Broccoli is also able to be eaten in a variety of delicious ways, such as with cream cheese, pepper paste, and butter, just to name a few. I recommend everybody to start eating more broccoli.

- Are You Healthy?
- The Best Vegetable
- Vegetables Are Good For our Health

LESSON 6 ANALYZING SENTENCES: I LIKE BADMINTON

(1) My partner, Charles, on the other hand, likes playing rugby best. (2) I, however, think rugby is too violent, and therefore is not good for your body. (3) Another reason I don't like rugby is that you must play it outside, and as a result weather can often affect your performance. (4) Finally, I don't like rugby because it is a team sport. (5) I only like to play individual sports. (6) While Charles may like rugby, I don't.

1. Read the paragraph above one more time. Try to make similar sentences using the words given below.

a. Warren / yoga Sentence (1)

____

b. strenuous / joints and muscles (2)

____

c. yoga / lay down on the floor / your clothes get dirty (3)

____

d. yoga / you can't talk while you are doing it (4)

____

e. activities / where you can be as loud as you want (5)

____

f. Warren / yoga (6)

____

LESSON 7 VOCABULARY FOCUS

1. Examine the use of each word or phrase underlined below and see if you can guess the meaning. If you are not sure of the meaning, ask a classmate or check your dictionary. Once you have found the meanings of all the words and phrases, create your own sentences with the bold-faced words and phrases.

a. Communist countries **frown on** self expression.

b. My parents have **no tolerance for** loud music.

c. My brother loves **competitive activities**.

d. A little **friendly competition** is good for everybody.

e. My history teacher's teaching style is very **dry**.

f. Drinking too much alcohol is **detrimental** to your health.

g. The music coming from the car was very **obscene**.

h. Coffee leaves a bad **after–taste** in your mouth.

i. Love stories are always so **predictable**.

a. ______________________________

b. ______________________________

c. ______________________________

d. ______________________________

e. ______________________________

f. ______________________________

g. ______________________________

h. ______________________________

i. ______________________________

LESSON 8 EXAMPLE PARAGRAPHS

I Like Music Better Than Math

I study many subjects in school, but here are three reasons why I like think music is the most interesting. Music class allows us to express ourselves through song, and as a result we can let others know how we feel and think. In addition, music class lets us interact with each other in both chorus and rhythm. Finally, music class is filled with variety. You can sit or stand, play an instrument or sing. The possibilities are endless. In my opinion, music is the best subject in school.

My friend, Yu-Jin, on the other hand, says that math is the most interesting subject in school. I, however, think math is very boring and difficult because I am not good at figures and understanding graphs. Another reason I don't think math is interesting is because in math there is no room for self expression. In math there is always one correct answer, and as a result there is no room for originality. Finally, math class is very monotonous, consisting only of day after day of problem solving with no variation. For these reasons I think music is more interesting than math.

Assignment

Using the example from page 62 you have to create a two paragraph story about something that you like more than something else. Sports, movies, food, etc. You will be graded according to the chart below. In addition, there should be no spelling mistakes. All spelling mistakes will result in an automatic 5 point deduction from your grade.

Followed the correct layout	/5
Had a well written title	/5
Had three or more well written supporting sentences	/5
Had well written concluding sentences	/5
Had at least two sentences connected with because	/5
Had two well written paragraphs, each consisting of their own connected topic	/5
Total Score	/30

Assignment Layout

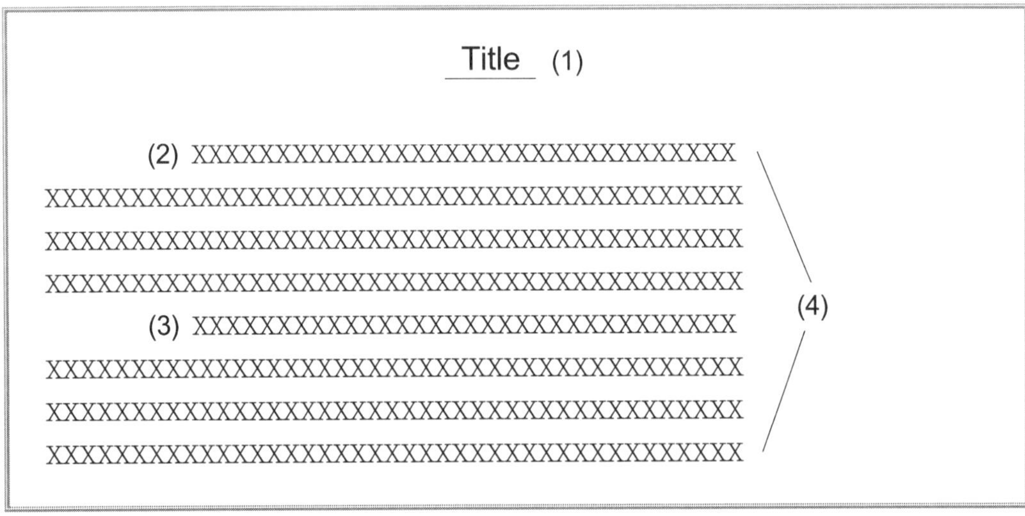

1. Your title should be in the center of your page and underlined. The first letter of your title should be capitalized.

2.–3. The first sentence of each paragraph should be indented.

4. The remaining sentences in your body should align on the right side of your page evenly. There should be two spaces between each line in your composition.

Self-Check List

1. Use the check-list below to make sure you have completed the assignment correctly.

Did you...	Yes	No
follow the correct layout?		
write a well written title?		
write three or more well written supporting sentences?		
write well written concluding sentences?		
write at least two sentences connected with because?		
write two well written paragraphs, each consisting of their own connected topic?		
make any spelling mistakes?		

Peer Review

1. Read your partner's assignment. Find your partner's topic sentences and write them below. Do you feel these are strong or weak topic sentences and why?

2. Choose one supporting sentence from each paragraph which you feel was most weakest. Please write them below.

3. Did you find any incorrect sentences or spelling mistakes? If so, please write them below.

4. Use the check-list below to make sure you partner has completed the assignment correctly.

Did your partner...	Yes	No
follow the correct layout?		
write a well written title?		
write three or more well written supporting sentences?		
write well written concluding sentences?		
write at least two sentences connected with because?		
write two well written paragraphs, each consisting of their own connected topic?		
make any spelling mistakes?		

5. Discuss your findings and results with your partner.

Writing Flow

Unit 05 Review

1. Please answer the following questions in full sentences.

a. What is a sentence?

b. What makes a basic sentence?

c. What is a Topic sentence ?

d. What is a Supporting sentence ?

e. What is a concluding sentence ?

2. Choose the correct lettered answer for each question below.

a. What do you like to do on the weekends?

(a) I like watch movies.
(b) I watching movies.
(c) I like to watch movies.
(d) I like to watch movie.

b. What does she like to do on Saturdays?

(a) She is like baseball.
(b) She is like playing baseball.
(c) She likes to play baseball.
(d) She liked to play baseball.

3. Which two sentences would be best connected with the word "but"?

(a) I like pork. I don't like chicken.

(b) I like beef. I like lamb.

(c) I don't like cities. I like reading books.

(d) I don't like baseball. I don't like tennis.

4. Which sentence below **is** grammatically correct?

a. (a) I like sports, because I like to exercise.

(b) I like sports because I like to exercise.

(c) I like sports because, I like to exercise.

(d) I like sports, because, I like to exercise.

b. (a) My friend thought her legs were ugly, and consequently she wouldn't wear skirts.

(b) My friend thought her legs were ugly, and, consequently she wouldn't wear skirts.

(c) My friend thought her legs were ugly and consequently she wouldn't wear skirts.

(d) My friend thought her legs were ugly and consequently, she wouldn't wear skirts.

c. (a) My brother thought he was stupid and therefore he didn't like to study.

(b) My brother thought he was stupid and therefore, he didn't like to study.

(c) My brother thought he was stupid, and therefore he didn't like to study.

(d) My brother thought he was stupid, therefore he didn't like to study.

d. (a) I finally decided to exercise. As a result, I have lost three kilograms.

(b) I finally decided to exercise as a result, I have lost three kilograms.

(c) I finally decided to exercise, as a result I have lost three kilograms.

(d) I finally decided to exercise. As a result I have lost three kilograms.

e. (a) I like cake, because I like sweet tasting food.

(b) I like cake because, I like sweet tasting food.

(c) I like cake because I like, sweet tasting food.

(d) I like cake because I like sweet tasting food.

5. Circle the letters that should be capitalized in the titles below.

a. the magnificent english teacher

b. knowledge of the unknown

c. crazy kung fu monkeys

d. a night in paradise

6. Match each word to its correct synonym.

a. after–taste

b. obscene

c. impeccable

d. lavish

e. reluctant

f. aspiring

g. acquainted

h. siblings

i. ambitious

j. familiar

k. brothers and sisters

l. hesitant

m. crude

n. Luxurious

o. perfect

p. persisting flavor

Unit 06 The Best Place On Earth!

▶ In this unit, you will learn how to ...

- make an *outline*
- write an *attention getter*
- write an *introductory paragraph*
- combine sentences with *so*
- remove clutter from your paragraphs
- use *a*, *an*, and *the* in sentences
- expand your vocabulary when writing

1. Read the composition on the next page. Next, discuss the meanings of any unfamiliar words or phrases, including the bold-faced words and phrases in the composition.
2. Ask your partner where they like to go to have fun in Korea.
3. Ask your partner what they do at the places they go to have fun.
4. Discuss with your partner a place you would recommend for a foreigner to go to have fun while they were in Korea.

At the end of this unit, you will be asked to write a four paragraph composition. The composition should detail a day trip to a place of your choosing in South Korea for a foreigner. The composition should be well written with a strong introductory paragraph.

Do You Want to Have Fun?

Here is a one day trip to Philadelphia that is sure to please you. You'll start with a morning boat tour, then go to a delicious cheese steak restaurant in the afternoon. Finally you will end your day **dancing the night away** at a world famous club. I am sure that you are going to have a great time.

We will start our day trip at the Hudson River. Here you will be able to take a boat ride around the city of Philadelphia. While you are riding in the boat, you will be able to admire Philadelphia's **historic architecture**, as well as see some famous modern places, such as Will Prince's house.

Riding on a boat all morning will surely make you hungry, so we will stop for lunch at Philly Joe's Cheese Steak House. This restaurant **overlooks** the Liberty Bell, yet is not expensive and has the best Philly cheese steaks in all of Philadelphia. Each cheese steak is made with five ounces of **freshly sliced** ground beef, two slices of cheese, lots of fried peppers, onions, and mushrooms on a toasted hoagie roll. I am sure you have never eaten anything as delicious as this before **in your life**.

After riding a boat and eating a delicious Philly cheese steak, it's time to dance the night away at the Boom Boom Club. The Boom Boom Club is famous for its great music and live caged tigers in the center of the dance floor. Combine these things with the Boom Boom Club's **reputation** for star **appearances** and I am sure you will have a **truly memorable** night.

LESSON 1 PRE WRITING AND BRAINSTORMING: MAKING AN OUTLINE

1. Think of some places that you like to go to. Next, think of what you like to do at each of the places that you chose.

Place	What I do there
Philadelphia	Take a boat ride

2. Once you have made a list of places that you like to go to, choose your favorite place and make an idea web on the next page of things you like to do there. Use the example below to help you get started.

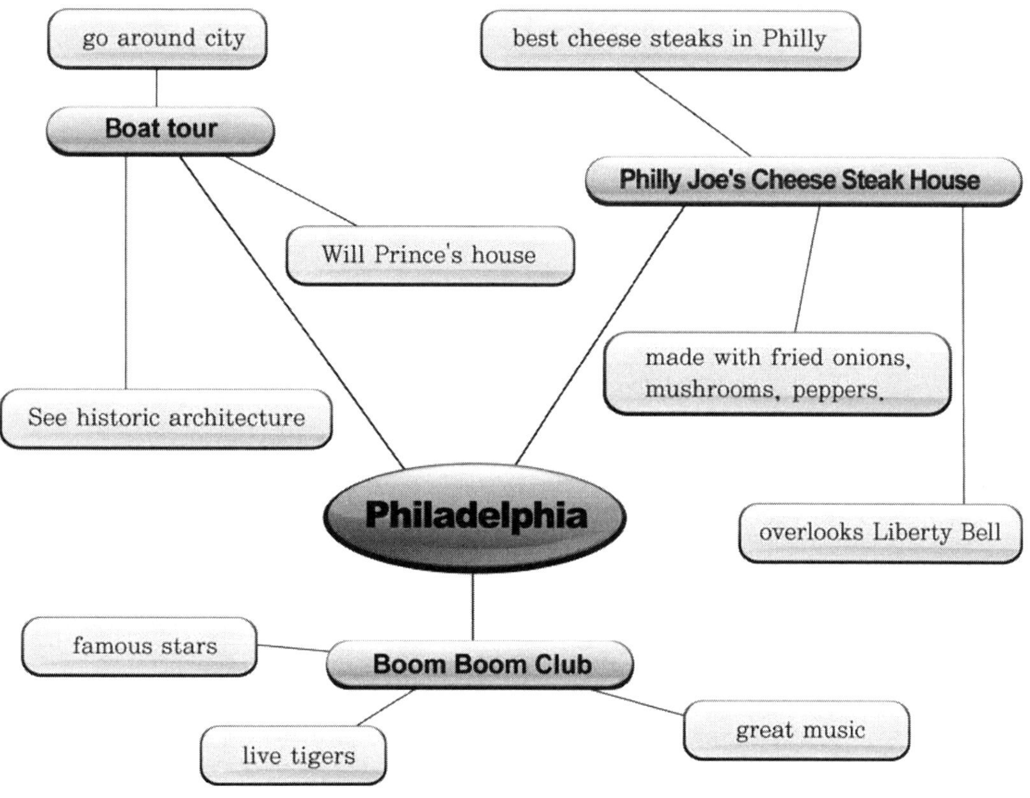

3.

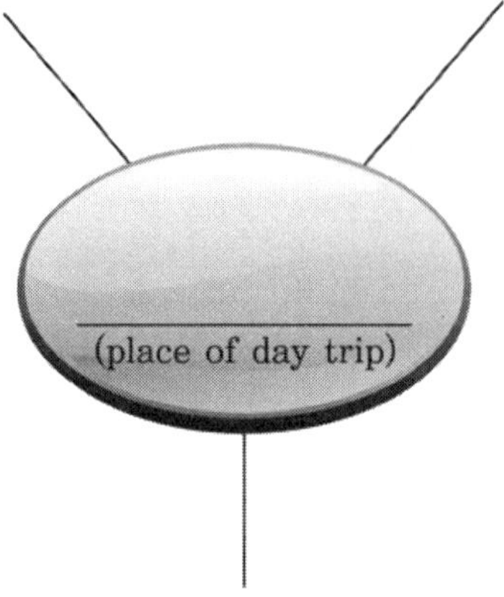

4. Once you have grouped your ideas together in an idea web, it is sometimes helpful to write these ideas out in outline form. Putting your ideas in outline form will allow you to present your ideas more clearly in paragraph form. To gain a better comprehension of this look at the example below.

Do you want to have fun?

1.0 Introductory paragraph

> Every composition will start with an introductory paragraph. This will be explained on pg. 78.

2.0 Boat tour

- On the boat tour you can travel around the city.
- On the boat tour you can see Philadelphia's historic architecture.
- On the boat tour you can see actor Will Prince's house.

3.0 Philly Joe's Cheese Steak House

- Philly Joe's Cheese Steak House overlooks the Liberty Bell.
- Philly Joe's has the best cheese steaks in all of Philadelphia.
- Philly Joe's cheese steaks are made with fried onions, mushrooms, and peppers.

4.0 Boom Boom Club

- The Boom Boom Club has great music.
- The Boom Boom Club has live tigers on the dance floor.
- Famous stars often come to the Boom Boom Club.

> Each sentence written under a numbered section will be a supporting sentence used in the composition for that paragraph.

> Each numbered line will represent one paragraph in your composition. The titles given to each numbered line will represent the main idea of each individual paragraph.

> Note that your outline should match your idea web.

go around city
boat tour
Will Prince's house
See historic architecture
best cheese steaks in Philly
Philly Joe's Cheese Steak House
made with fried onions, mushrooms, peppers.
overlooks Liberty Bell
Philadelphia
famous stars
Boom Boom Club
live tigers
great music

5. Using the idea web and the example from the previous page, try to make your own outline below.

1.0 Introductory paragraph

____

____

2.0 ____

- ______________________________
- ______________________________
- ______________________________
- ______________________________

3.0 ____

- ______________________________
- ______________________________
- ______________________________
- ______________________________

4.0 ____

- ______________________________
- ______________________________
- ______________________________
- ______________________________

LESSON 2 WRITING FOCUS: ATTENTION GETTERS

An ***attention getter*** appears as the **title of a composition.** The purpose of an attention getter is to get the reader **interested** in the story that they are about to read.

Types of Attention Getters:

※ can be a sentence, a question, quote, or just one word.

※ are often surprising, funny, or make you think about a problem you have.

※ sometimes are accompanied by a picture.

ex. (Sentence) Let's get rich together!

(Question) Do you want to speak English perfectly?

(Word) Unbelievable!

(Quote) "It's not what you know, it's who you know."

1. Try to write your own attention getter for each item below.

a. (a pair of shoes)

____

b. (a trip to Jeju Island)

____

c. (a new sports drink called "Sport Fuel")

____

LESSON 3 WRITING FOCUS: INTRODUCTORY PARAGRAPHS

An ***introductory paragraph*** begins a composition and often contains these three things……

1. The main Idea:

A sentence or set of sentences stating the main topic or thesis of the composition. In other words, a sentence or set of sentences telling the reader why you wrote this composition.

2. The preview:

A list of the points that will be discussed, showing the reader the organization and flow of the composition.

3. A concluding sentence:

A sentence summarizing the main idea of the paragraph.

Note After reading the introductory paragraph the reader should know exactly what will appear in the composition they are about to read.

1. Follow the directions below for each letter.

a. Rewrite the **main idea** of the paragraph below.

If you would like to be rich, then here is the way – the Money Tree. Becoming rich with the Money Tree just takes three easy steps. First, you must plant the tree in your house. Second, you must water it everyday with a special solution. Finally, you must place the tree under a special ultraviolet light. In this article, I will teach you how to follow these three easy steps to become rich with the Money Tree. The Money Tree is an excellent way to get rich fast.

____

____

b. Rewrite the **first sentence of the preview** in the paragraph below.

There are three things you must think about when choosing clothes for a job interview: color, style, and comfort. In this article I will tell you first what colors work best with what type of interview. Next, I will tell you which style clothes are best to wear depending on the interview. Last, I will tell you about the importance of comfort when attending a job interview. Being aware of the color, style, and comfort of your clothes when going to a job interview will help you land your next job.

____

____

c. Rewrite the **last sentence of the preview** in the paragraph below.

Brazil is a great place to spend your next vacation. You can find relaxing beaches, excellent shopping areas, and an exciting night life. As a native of Brazil, in this article I will first tell you where the best beaches are. Next, I will give you information on the best shopping areas, and finally I will teach you how to experience the most exciting night life in the world. This is going to be the best vacation you have ever had.

____

____

Here is a one day trip to Philadelphia that is sure to please you. You'll start with a morning boat tour, then go to a delicious cheese steak restaurant in the afternoon. Finally, you will end your day dancing your night away at a world famous club. I am sure that you are going to have a great time.

2. Using the example above try to write your own introductory paragraph for a special place in South Korea.

a. Attention Getter: ______________________________

b. Main Idea: ______________________________

c. Preview: ______________________________

____

____

____

d. Concluding Sentence (optional) ______________________________

____

LESSON 4 LANGUAGE FOCUS: COMBING SENTENCES WITH SO

To show a result, combine sentences with the word ***so***. Use a comma after the first sentence and before so.

ex.

Sentence #1	Sentence #2
I think Dave likes Italian food.	I would like to take him to an Italian restaurant.

I think Dave likes Italian food, ***so*** I would like to take him to an Italian restaurant.

1. Connect the sentences below using the word so.

a. I lived in New Zealand for 3 years. I can speak English well.

____

b. I think dancing is so much fun. I like going to night clubs.

____

c. You look hungry. Let's get something to eat.

____

d. You like pizza. Why don't we go to Pizza Mama?

____

LESSON 5 ORGANIZATION FOCUS: REMOVING CLUTTER

Removing clutter is the process of checking your composition for any off topic ideas or sentences unrelated to the topic sentence of your paragraph or story, and then removing them. Practicing good pre–writing and brain storming techniques can often help eliminate off topic ideas and sentences in compositions. However, it never hurts to read over a composition several times before submitting it, double checking it for any off topic ideas and sentences. Learning to remove clutter can significantly improve the clarity, as well as the quality, of your work.

1. Read the composition below and cross out any off topic ideas or sentences.

Experience the Beauty of London

Here is a one day trip to London that is sure to please you. You'll start with a morning tour of Buckingham Palace, then go to the famous Tower of London in the afternoon. Finally you will end your day relaxing at a world famous English pub. I am sure that you are going to have a great time.

We will start our day trip at Buckingham Palace. Here you will be able to watch the internationally famous changing of the guard. In London it often rains, so you should bring a rain jacket. Watching the changing of the guard is certainly exciting. Next, we will visit the nineteen State Rooms. The nineteen State Rooms are elegantly decorated with antique art and furniture to awe you. After watching the changing of the guard and viewing the nineteen State Rooms we will end our tour of Buckingham Palace with a view of the garden. Buckingham Palace's garden is the largest private garden in London. My girlfriend thinks that this garden is very beautiful.

After Buckingham Palace we will head to the Tower of London. At the Tower of London we first take a tour of the White Tower, which was built by William the Conqueror. William the Conqueror was the King of England from 1066 to 1087. His reign brought Norman French culture to England. In the White Tower you will have a chance to view Norman Chapel of St. John, which is one of the finest examples of Norman church architecture in the world. Next, we will move along to the Royal Armory, where you can see ancient weapons of war. Last, we will view the Crown

Jewels.

A full morning and afternoon of sightseeing will make you want to relax. The Queen's Pub is famous for its great beer and friendly atmosphere. Sometimes the Queen's Pub is very loud, so if you don't like loud places you might want to try a different pub. Besides great beer and a friendly atmosphere the Queen's Pub also has delicious fish and chips to satisfy your appetite. Everybody in England likes to eat fish and chips. Combine these things with the Queen's Pub's club's live band and I am sure you will have a truly memorable day.

LESSON 6 LANGUAGE FOCUS: USING THE ARTICLES "A", "AN", & "THE"

Use ***the*** when the reader already recognizes the specific person, place, or thing you are writing about.

ex. I walked out of ***the*** house and towards ***the*** playground.

We also use ***the*** when we go to a place for another reason other than the reason we usually go there for.

ex. I have to go to ***the*** school.

Use ***a*** and ***an*** when you are mentioning **a person**, **place**, or **thing** for the first time and ***the*** when you mention it again.

ex. Our dorm has ***a*** sports center. ***The*** sports center is free.

Use ***a*** and ***an*** to refer to something in general.

ex. It's fun to be ***a*** student.
She has ***an*** apple.

http://blog.naver.com/shinsa2080

1. Using the information and examples from the previous page, try to complete the paragraph below using *a*, *an*, and *the*.

An Amazing College

Let me tell you about _________college in Germany. _________name of ___________college is Berlin Technical College –BTC. BTC is _____ big college located in ________center of Berlin, Germany. It has huge dormitories that are beautifully decorated. Most of ________students at BTC live in them. Each dorm floor has it's own bathroom which includes twelve individual showers, twelve toilets, _____sauna, as well as ____spa.

BTC gets better. BTC has one of _______best cafeterias in all of Germany. _______ cafeteria is set up buffet style, with a variety of different foods to choose from. There is ______ Italian corner, French, Japanese, Chinese, and even _____ Greek corner.

By far _______ students' favorite place on campus is _______ student lounge. The BTC student lounge is fully equipment to help students study, as well as relax, all in one convenient place. ______ BTC lounge has five 60inch TV's, _____ singing room, billiards room, game room, and ________ snack bar.

Everyone that attends BTC agrees that BTC is the best college in all of Germany.

LESSON 7 VOCABULARY PRACTICE

1. Examine the use of each underlined word or phrase below and see if you can guess the meaning. If you are not sure of the meaning, ask a classmate or check your dictionary. Once you have found the meanings of all the words and phrases, create your own sentences with the bold-faced words and phrases.

   a. Let's **head to** the coffee shop.

   b. You can party **all night long**.

   c. At the shopping mall you can buy various **knick-knacks**.

   d. The food here is **mouth-watering**.

   e. The restaurant has a **warm atmosphere**.

   f. This tower **gives off a romantic vibe** for couples.

   g. The mountain is **truly breathtaking**.

   h. You can **take a break** at the park.

   i. This shop has a lot of very **good deals**.

   a. ______________________________

   b. ______________________________

   c. ______________________________

   d. ______________________________

   e. ______________________________

   f. ______________________________

   g. ______________________________

   h. ______________________________

   i. ______________________________

LESSON 8 EXAMPLE

Come Experience Insadong!

Written below is a one day trip to Insadong that is sure to please you. You'll start with a morning of shopping, then go to a famous Korean dumpling restaurant, and finally end your day winding down over a delicious cup of Korean traditional tea. It's going to be a blast!

Introductory Paragraph

We will start at the Insadong Souvenir Mall. Here you will be able to buy various Korean souvenirs for your friends and family. Some popular souvenirs include traditional Korean masks, chopstick sets, and beautifully hand painted Korean fans.

Morning Activity

Shopping will make you hungry, so you should find a place to eat. I suggest "Big Grandmother's Dumpling House". It's not expensive and it has the best handmade dumplings in all of Korea. Not to mention, all of the ingredients used are organic, so besides the taste it is also healthy for you.

Afternoon Activity

After a full morning of shopping and a delicious lunch, it's time to relax and reminisce on your great day in Insadong. A nice cup of Korean ginseng tea at "Flying Bird Tea Shop" will relax your body and re-energize you after a long day. Besides the great tea and relaxing time, "Flying Bird Tea Shop" is famous for it's live birds flying in the shop.

Evening Activity

Assignment

Using the example from page 87 you have to create a four paragraph day trip to a place of your choosing in South Korea. In addition to an Introductory paragraph, you should include a morning, afternoon, and evening activity in your composition. You will be graded according to the chart below. In addition, there should be no spelling mistakes. All spelling mistakes will result in an automatic 5 point deduction from your grade.

Followed the correct layout	/5
Had a well written **attention getter**	/5
Had a well written introductory paragraph	/5
Had a well written morning, afternoon, and evening paragraph	/5
Used the word **so** to connect two or more sentences	/5
Correctly used **a**, **an**, and **the** articles	/5
Total Score	/30

Assignment Layout

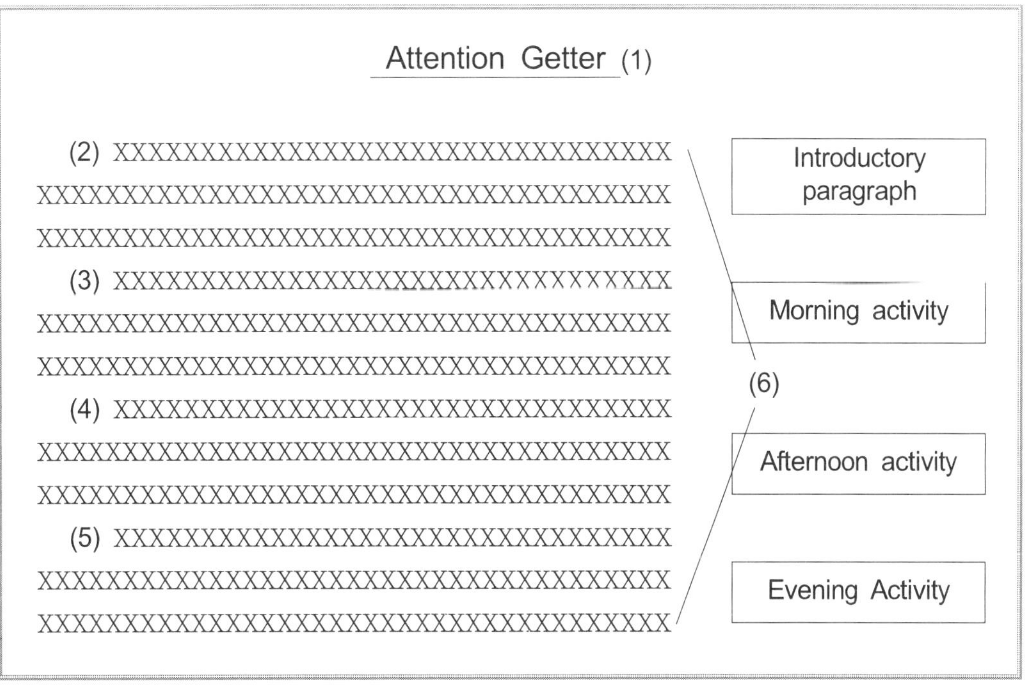

1. Your "attention getter" should be in the center of your page, underlined, and capitalized correctly.

2.-5. The first sentence of each paragraph should be indented. Paragraph (2) should be your introductory paragraph. Paragraph (3) should be your morning activity. Paragraph (4) should be your afternoon activity, and paragraph (5) should be your evening activity.

6. The remaining sentences in your body should align on the right side of your page evenly. There should be two spaces between each line in your composition.

Self-Check List

1. Use the check-list below to make sure you have completed the assignment correctly.

Did you...	Yes	No
follow the correct layout?		
write a well written attention getter?		
write a well written introductory paragraph?		
write a well written morning, afternoon, and evening paragraph?		
use the word "so" to connect two or more sentences?		
correctly use *a*, *an*, and *the* articles?		
make any spelling mistakes?		

Peer Review

1. Read your partner's assignment. Did your partner write a clear preview in their introductory paragraph. Below, please write what you will do in the morning, afternoon and evening, based on your partner's introductory paragraph.

2. Choose one supporting sentence from each paragraph which you feel best supports that sentence's topic sentence. Please write them below.

3. Did you find any incorrect sentences or spelling mistakes? If so, please write them below.

4. Use the check-list below to make sure your partner has completed the assignment correctly.

Did your partner...	Yes	No
follow the correct layout?		
write a well written attention getter?		
write a well written introductory paragraph?		
write a well written morning, afternoon, and evening paragraph?		
use the word so to connect two or more sentences?		
correctly use **a**, **an**, and **the** articles?		
make any spelling mistakes?		

5. Discuss your findings and results with your partner.

Unit 07 Which One is Better?

▶ In this unit, you will learn how to ...

- use freewriting to help organize your thoughts and ideas
- write a concluding paragraph
- use the word ***unlike*** to link sentences
- use the expression ***on the other hand*** to link sentences
- use ***however*** , ***whereas*** , and ***while*** to link sentences
- organize a point by point comparison composition
- expand your vocabulary when writing

1. Read the composition on the next page. Next, discuss the meanings of any unfamiliar words or phrases, including the bold-faced words and phrases in the composition on the next page.

2. With your partner, look at the picture pairs above. Discuss which item in the pair you like most, and why.

At the end of this unit, you will be asked to write a three paragraph composition, contrasting two things of your choosing. The composition should be well written with a strong introductory paragraph, point-by-point comparison body, and concluding paragraph.

My Preference Between Dogs and Cats

Dogs and cats are common pets ***throughout the world***, but which is better? Some people say that dogs make the best pets, others say cats. In this composition, I will explain why dogs are better pets than cats.

There are three main reasons why dogs are better than cats. First, dogs are fun and energetic. People can play, exercise, and enjoy life together with dogs. Cats, on the other hand, are very boring and lazy, making playing games and exercising with them almost impossible. Can you imagine playing catch with a cat? Next, dogs can be trained to go to the bathroom outside, which keeps our houses cleaner and smelling better. Cats, however, go to the bathroom in a ***litter box***, making our houses smell and seem dirty. Finally, dogs listen better than cats. If you call a dog's name, usually it will come to you. If you tell a dog to sit, it usually will. Cats, in comparison, don't even know their own names. You could call a cat all day long and it would never come to you.

Dogs are easier to ***interact with***, they keep our houses smelling and looking better, not to mention they are better listeners. It seems clear that dogs are much better pets than cats.

LESSON 1 WRITING FOCUS: PRE-WRITING AND BRAINSTORMING

1. Try to think of as many opposites as possible.

Item 1	Item 2
Dogs	Cats

2. Looking at the list above, choose the pair of opposites that you like best. For the next five minutes write as much about that pair as you can without stopping. This brainstorming technique is called **freewriting**.

LESSON 2 WRITING FOCUS: CONCLUDING PARAGRAPHS

A concluding paragraph is the last paragraph of a composition. The purpose of a concluding paragraph is to bring your composition to a logical end. There are three basic types of concluding paragraphs generally used in academic writing.

(Summary) repeats the main points of the composition.
(Prediction) discusses what will happen in the future.
(Evaluation) compares the main points and states what is best.

1. Below are 3 concluding paragraphs of the same topic. Try to decide which style each paragraph follows. Is it a summary, prediction, or an evaluation paragraph?

a. As we have seen, both cars and motorcycles have advantages as well as disadvantages. But which is better? Cars are good for bad weather and storage, while motorcycles help people avoid traffic and arrive on time. As mentioned previously, however, in recent years increased traffic congestion, and the demand to be on time, has caused more and more people to buy motorcycles. For this reason, in twenty years motorcycles will be more popular than cars among teenagers, as well as adults.

____

b. In conclusion, due to increased traffic congestion, as well as the demand to be on time, motorcycles are becoming more and more popular. This has led teenagers, as well as adults, to buy motorcycles instead of cars.

____

c. Therefore, if you are considering buying a motorcycle or a car, think about your needs. If you are a person who needs to be on time and dislikes traffic, the answer is clear. It is better to buy a motorcycle instead of a car.

____

LESSON 3 LANGUAGE FOCUS: USING "UNLIKE"

We can use the word ***unlike*** to describe a difference between nouns.

Dogs, unlike cats, are very fun and energetic.

Notice in the example above. That when ***unlike*** is used to compare two nouns, a comma must be placed after the first noun and before ***unlike***. In addition, a comma must be placed after the noun that proceeds the word ***unlike***.

1. For each letter below, use ***unlike*** to make a comparative sentence that includes the words given below.

   a. High School / University

   ____

   b. Winter / Summer

   ____

   c. Pen / Pencil

   ____

   d. Babies / Adults

   ____

LESSON 4 LANGUAGE FOCUS: USING "ON THE OTHER HAND"

We can use ***On the other hand*** to start a new sentence, which is in opposition to the sentence that proceeded it.

In the summer it is hot. On the other hand, winter is cold.

Notice in the example above. That when ***on the other hand*** is used to start a sentence it must be followed by a comma.

1. For each letter below, use *on the other hand* to make a comparative sentence that includes the words given below.

a. Socks / Gloves

____

b. Boys / Girls

____

c. South Korea / North Korea

____

d. Christian / Buddhist

____

LESSON 5 LANGUAGE FOCUS: USING "HOWEVER"

However can be used to connect a new sentence to a proceeding sentence of opposition. **If *however* begins a sentence it must be followed by a comma.**
ex. Boys like to play sports. However, girls like to watch soap operas.

However can also be used to join two sentences of opposing ideas. If "however" is used in this manner **it must be proceeded by a semi-colon and followed by a comma.**
ex. Boys like to play sports; however, girls like to watch soap operas.

However can be used to interrupt a sentence to add emphasis. If "however" is use to interrupt a sentence **it must be off set by commas.**
ex. Boys like to play sports. Girls, however, like to watch soap operas.

1. For each letter below, use however to make a comparative sentence.

a. Going to the movie theater is very expensive.
Watching a DVD at home is very cheap.

____

b. My friends like to play basketball.
I like to play soccer.

____

c. Mr. Burns gives a lot of homework.
Mrs. Wilson hardly ever gives homework.

____

LESSON 6 LANGUAGE FOCUS: USING "WHEREAS" AND "WHILE"

Whereas can be used to combine two opposite ideas into one sentence. **If *whereas* begins a sentence no comma is used. A comma, however, must be used to separate the ideas.**

ex. Whereas math is very difficult, history is very easy.

Whereas can also be used to join two sentences of opposing ideas. However, the word ***while*** is more commonly used. When while is used to connect two sentences **it must be proceeded by a comma.**

ex. Math is very difficult, while history is very easy.

1. Read the paragraph below. Following the rules from lessons 3, 4, 5, and 6 add commas so that it is grammatically correct.

There are three reasons why Christmas is better than Halloween. First, on Christmas we don't have to go to school on the other hand on Halloween we do. Second, on Christmas we receive presents from our friends and family while on Halloween we only get candy. Once our candy is eaten it can no longer bring us pleasure. Presents however can give us pleasure for years and years. Finally, Christmas lights unlike Halloween decorations are very beautiful. Looking at Christmas lights makes people feel alive and merry while looking at Halloween decorations makes people feel sad and depressed. Whereas some people like Halloween I like Christmas.

LESSON 7 ORGANIZATION FOCUS: WRITING POINT-BY-POINT COMPARISON PARAGRAPHS

One way to organize comparison paragraphs is by using a ***point-by-point layout***. When using a point-by-point layout, each sentence in your paragraph is written in opposition to either its preceeding or following sentence.

1. To better understand how to use a point-by-point layout, look at the example below.

(1) There are three major differences between the versatility and convenience of digital and film cameras. (2) First, when using a digital camera we can immediately check to see if we have taken a good picture or not. (3) With film cameras, however, we don't know if the picture we took was good or not until we develop it. (4) Second, digital pictures can be sent to friends and family within minutes of taking a picture. (5) On the other hand, we have to wait several hours before we can send pictures taken by film cameras. (6) Last, with most digital cameras, aside from pictures, we can also make movies. (7) Whereas film cameras have no such function. (8) It seems that digital cameras are more versatile and convenient than film cameras.

Introductory sentence

First point about digital cameras.

First point about film cameras.

Second point about digital cameras.

Second point about film cameras.

Third point about digital cameras.

Third point about film cameras.

Concluding sentence

LESSON 8 VOCABULARY FOCUS

1. Examine the use of each underlined word or phrase below and see if you can guess the meaning. If you are not sure of the meaning, ask a classmate or check your dictionary. Once you have found the meanings of all the words and phrases, create your own sentences with the bold-faced words and phrases.

   a. Laptops are more **versatile** than standard computers.

   b. Cell–phones are more **convenient** than pay phones.

   c. Motorcycles are more **affordable** than cars.

   d. Name brand products are more reliable than **generic brand products**.

   e. Parking downtown is always such a **hassle**.

   f. His shoes are very **durable**.

   g. I always buy **knock–off** clothes, because they are cheaper.

   h. I want to move to a more **spacious** apartment.

   i. He has an **extensive** library.

   a. ______________________________

   b. ______________________________

   c. ______________________________

   d. ______________________________

   e. ______________________________

   f. ______________________________

   g. ______________________________

   h. ______________________________

   i. ______________________________

LESSON 9 EXAMPLE

Where do you live? People live all over the world. Some people live in cities, others live in the country. Some people say that country life is the best life, but I disagree. I think that the best place to live is in a city.	**Introductory Paragraph**
I have lived in both the country and the city. Cities are filled with life and excitement. Whereas the country is boring and dull. Cities have excellent schools to educate people, unlike the country, which can barely provide a basic education for people. Cities provide numerous job opportunities. On the other hand, people that live in the country often can't find work. People that live in the country usually come to the city to work.	**Main Body point-by-point comparison**
In conclusion, a city provides more excitement, a better education, as well as better job opportunities than the country. It is clear that living in the city is better than living in the country.	**Concluding Paragraph**

Assignment

Using the example from page 102 you have to create a three paragraph composition in which you compare two things. You will be graded according to the chart below. In addition, there should be no spelling mistakes. All spelling mistakes will result in an automatic 5 point deduction from your grade.

Followed the correct layout	/5
Wrote a well written introductory paragraph	/5
Wrote a point-by-point comparison main body paragraph	/5
Wrote a well written concluding paragraph	/5
Wrote sentences using **however**, **while**, or **whereas.**	/5
Wrote sentences using **unlike** or **on the other hand**	/5
Total Score	/30

Assignment Layout

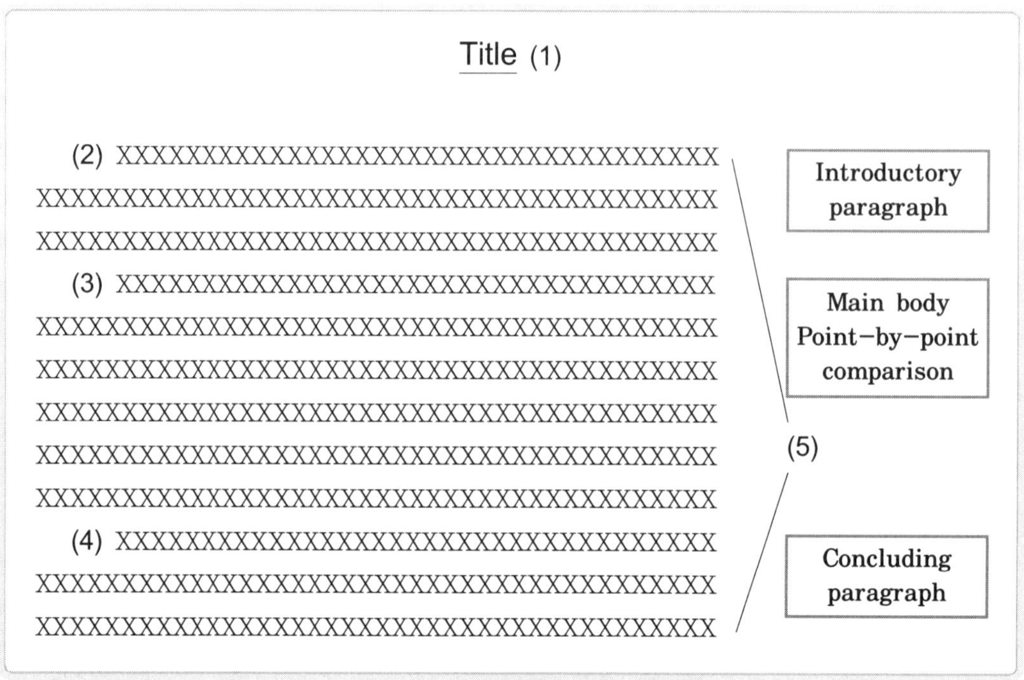

1. Your title should be in the center of your page, underlined, and capitalized correctly.

2.–5. The first sentence of each paragraph should be indented. Paragraph (2) should be your introductory paragraph. Paragraph (3) should be your main body point-by-point comparison. Paragraph (4) should be your concluding paragraph.

6. The remaining sentences in your body should align on the right side of your page evenly. There should be two spaces between each line in your composition.

Self–Check List

1. Use the check-list below to make sure you have completed the assignment correctly.

Did you...	Yes	No
follow the correct layout?		
write a well written introductory paragraph?		
write a point–by–point comparison main body paragraph?		
write a well written concluding paragraph?		
write sentences using ***however***, ***while***, or ***whereas***?		
write sentences using ***unlike*** or ***on the other hand***?		
make any spelling mistakes?		

Peer Review

1. Read your partner's assignment. Did your partner write a well written concluding paragraph? Summarize your partner's conclusion below.

2. Read your partner's main body. What three points of comparison did your partner use to support their concluding paragraph? Please summarize them below.

3. Did you find any incorrect sentences or spelling mistakes? If so, please write them below.

4. Use the check-list below to make sure your partner has completed the assignment correctly.

Did your partner...	Yes	No
follow the correct layout?		
write a well written introductory paragraph?		
write a point-by-point comparison main body paragraph?		
write a well written concluding paragraph?		
write sentences using ***however***, ***while***, or ***whereas***?		
write sentences using ***unlike*** or ***on the other hand***?		
make any spelling mistakes?		

5. Discuss your findings and results with your partner.

Writing Flow

Unit 08 It's a Must See!

▶ **In this unit, you will learn how to ...**

- write a multi–paragraph movie review
- use apostrophes to show possession
- expand your vocabulary

1. Read the composition on the next page. Next, discuss the meanings of any unfamiliar words or phrases, including the bold-faced words and phrases in the composition.

2. What are the names of some movies that you have seen recently?

※ ______________________________

※ ______________________________

※ ______________________________

3. Discuss with your partner some of the best and worst movies that you both have seen.

Best Movies	Worst Movies

4. Discuss with your partner what you feel makes a good movie.

At the end of this unit, you will be asked to write a three paragraph movie review about a movie of your choosing. Each paragraph should be well written following the outline presented in this unit.

Dreaming of Taekkyon

Dreaming of Taekkyon tells the story of a young **aspiring** martial artist in **modern day** South Korea. Joon Ho Kim plays Hyun Bin Park, a high school student, who's dream is to become a famous Taekkyon master. The problem is Hyun Bin's parents, played by Chul Su Park and Tae Hee Do, think studying Taekkyon is a **waste of time**. Hyun Bin, however, is determined to become a famous martial artist regardless of his parents' opinion about Taekkyon. In the end, Hyun Bin's parents recognize his **passion** for Taekkyon and understand how much he loves doing it.

The message of *Dreaming of Taekkyon* is that you should follow your dream. In the movie, Hyun Bin is constantly **pressured** by his parents to stop practicing Taekkyon. While most people would have **given in** to the pressure, Hyun Bin never **gives up** on his dream of becoming a Taekkyon master.

In my opinion, *Dreaming of Taekkyon* was a great movie. It was **uplifting** and **inspiring**, teaching us the importance of **determination** and **dedication**. The characters were believable and well cast. I liked how Hyun Bin **dealt with** his parents' opposition to his dream. He was strong yet polite. I think that everybody should see this wonderful movie.

LESSON 1 WRITING FOCUS: PRE-WRITING AND BRAINSTORMING

1. Choose a movie to write a review about. While thinking of this movie, answer the questions below.

a. Who were the main characters in the movie? Who were they played by?

Movie character's name:	Actor or actress' name:
1.	1.
2.	2.
3.	3.
4.	4.

b. What was the movie's plot?

c. What was the message of the movie?

d. Would you recommend this movie to somebody else? Why or why not?

LESSON 2 ORGANIZATION FOCUS: THE PARTS OF A MOVIE REVIEW

Flight 445 Going Down

Title

Flight 445 Going Down is a movie about an airplane that crashes into the ocean. Based on a true story, the main character James Bison, played by Robin Willis, along with his wife Vivian, played by Kelly Khan, and son Webster, played by Jared McCoy, board a plane headed for sunny Hawaii. The Bison family is anticipating a fun two week winter vacation, when suddenly something goes terribly wrong. Lightening strikes the plane causing it to lose power and eventually crash into the Pacific Ocean. After hours of struggling in the cold ocean water, in the end, James is the only member of his family that survives.

First paragraph

The message of *Flight 445 Going Down* is that we should never take our loved ones for granted. In the movie, James, a workaholic, often neglects to show his family how much he loves them. In the end, he never gets the chance to tell them how much he loves them before they die.

Second paragraph

In my opinion, *Flight 445 Going Down* was a terrible movie. It was sad and depressing, constantly reminding us of how unfair life can be. The special effects were poorly done and the acting was terrible. I didn't like James' performance. It seemed fake and not heartfelt. I would not recommend this movie to others.

Third paragraph

> Notice that the main title of the movie review is written in bold-faced type and underlined. However, when the movie title appears in the proceeding paragraphs, it is italicized.

LESSON 3 ORGANIZATION FOCUS: THE FIRST PARAGRAPH

The first paragraph of a movie review usually:

- gives the reader an overview of the movie's setting
- gives the reader a brief introduction of the main characters in the movie, as well as the actors and actresses that play them.
- gives the reader a brief synopsis of the movie

Flight 445 Going Down is a movie about an airplane that crashes into the ocean.

The introductory sentence lets the reader know that the movie is set on an airplane.

Based on a true story, the main character James Bison, played by Robin Willis, along with his wife Vivian, played by Kelly Khan, and son Webster, played by Jared McCoy, board a plane headed for sunny Hawaii.

The following sentences introduce the main characters, as well as the real names of the actors and actresses that play them in the movie

The Bison family is anticipating a fun two week winter vacation, when suddenly something goes terribly wrong. Lightening strikes the plane causing it to lose power and eventually crash into the Pacific Ocean. After hours of struggling in the cold ocean water, in the end, James is the only member of his family that survives.

beginning

middle

end

The following sentences give the reader a brief synopsis of the movie from beginning to end.

LESSON 4 ORGANIZATION FOCUS: THE SECOND PARAGRAPH

The second paragraph of a movie review usually:

- tells the reader what the movie's main message is

The message of ***Flight 445 Going Down*** is that we should never take our loved ones for granted.

The introductory sentences of the second paragraph states the movies main message. In this example, **we should never take our loved ones for granted**, is the main message of the movie.

In the movie, James, a workaholic, often neglects to show his family how much he loves them. In the end, he never gets the chance to tell them how much he loves them before they die.

After the main message is stated, the remaining sentences in the paragraph provide an example from the movie that supports the main message.

LESSON 5 ORGANIZATION FOCUS: THE THIRD PARAGRAPH

The third paragraph of a movie review usually:

- discusses the quality of the movie and the acting.
- gives a recommendation as to whether the reader should or should not see the movie

In my opinion, ***Flight 445 Going Down*** was a terrible movie. It was sad and depressing, constantly reminding us of how unfair life can be. The special effects were poorly done and the acting was terrible. I didn't like James' performance. It seemed fake and not heartfelt.

opinion and quality of movie

Acting quality and supporting example

The introductory sentences of the third paragraph state the author's overall opinion of the movie. Next, the quality of the movie is further analyzed. After that, the acting in the movie is addressed and supported by a specific example. In the example above, the supporting sentences are:

"I didn't like James' performance. It seemed fake and not heartfelt."

I would not recommend this movie to others.

The concluding sentence of the paragraph tells the reader in plain words if they should or should not watch the reviewed movie.

1. Read the sentences below. Decide if they belong in the first, second, or third paragraph of a movie review.

ex.	I highly recommend this movie. ____Third Paragraph____

a. A professional baseball player, played by Wes Nelson.

____

b. Without warning, a deadly virus breaks out in the city.

____

c. Labeled as a comedy, the main actors in this movie were not funny at all.

____

d. This movie teaches us that money doesn't equal happiness.

____

LESSON 6 LANGUAGE FOCUS: USING APOSTROPHES

When writing, apostrophes are used to show a common noun or proper noun possession of something.

ex.

Common noun	The tree's leaves were red and yellow.
Proper noun	Sue's book bag was under the desk.

In cases where a singular common noun, proper noun, and a pronoun possess something, we can simply add an apostrophe and a "s" to show possession.

ex.

Common noun	The cat's fur was all over the floor.
Proper noun	Mike's hat was ugly.

In cases where plural common nouns and proper nouns which end in "s" possess something, we can simply add an apostrophe to the end of the word to show possession.

ex.

Plural common noun	The buses' wheels were dirty.
Proper noun	The Jones' house was huge.

Note 1 Although it is possible, as well as grammatically correct to add an apostrophe to a plural common noun to show possession, it is not common. It is more common to simply reverse the order of the sentence and inserting the word "of".

ex.

Plural common noun with apostrophe	The houses' roofs were old.
Reversed sentence	The roofs of the house were old.

Note 2 Correctly showing a common, plural common, or proper noun's possession of a common noun or material noun is often easy. However showing a common, plural common, or proper noun's possession of an abstract noun can often be confusing.

Common noun	The girl's attitude was terrible.
Plural common noun	The clothes' smell filled the room.
Proper noun	The Simpsons' confidence was unbelievable.

1. Using pg. 115 as a guide, correct the movie review below adding apostrophes where needed.

The Magic Book

The Magic Book tells the story of a young girls amazing book. Ye–Jin Cho plays Sung Ju Do, an elementary school student who finds a magic book in her school library. At first, Sung Ju book is a tremendous help. The problem is soon Sung Ju teachers find out that Sung Ju book, and not Sung Ju herself, has been doing her homework. Soon Sung Ju guilt makes her realize that she should destroy the book. However the book power is too strong and she is unable to destroy the book by herself. In the end, with the help of Sung Ju friends and family, she eventually destroys the book

The message of ***The Magic Book*** is that cheaters never win. In the movie, Sung Ju thinks that by cheating her life would be better, but in the end it only becomes worse.

In my opinion, ***The Magic Book*** was a great movie. It was educational and energetic, teaching us the importance of self motivation hard work. The characters were believable and well cast. I liked how Sung Ju dealt with the struggle between the book power and her parents and teachers pleas to destroy the book. She was sincere and heartfelt. I think that everybody should see this wonderful movie.

LESSON 7 VOCABULARY FOCUS

1. Examine the use of each word or phrase underlined below, and see if you can guess the meaning. If you are not sure of the meaning, ask a classmate or check your dictionary. Once you have found the meanings of all the words and phrases, create your own sentences with the bold-faced words and phrases.

a. I don't like **gory** movies.

b. Children shouldn't watch **explicit** movies.

c. That movie had a good **score**.

d. The movie had a very **imaginative** plot.

e. I don't like **slow-moving** films.

f. I love **action-packed** movies, like Alien Attack.

g. I found the acting in the movie to be very **offensive** towards Italians.

h. I was **in suspense** the whole time I watched the movie.

i. I found the movie to be a **real dud**.

a. ______________________________

b. ______________________________

c. ______________________________

d. ______________________________

e. ______________________________

f. ______________________________

g. ______________________________

h. ______________________________

i. ______________________________

LESSON 8 EXAMPLE

Love in Seoul

Love in Seoul tells the story of two students' summer vacation in Seoul, South Korea. Travis Perry and Angelina Jones, play two college students, Rob and Nita, who find themselves alone and lost on the crowded streets of Seoul. While the two try to find their classmates, they realize that they have a lot in common. After several discussions and some crazy events, they fall in love with each other. In the end, the two reunite with their classmates and return to the United States. To everyone's surprise, one month later, Rob dies in a car crash, leaving Nita with only the memories of their summer in Seoul.

The message of ***Love in Seoul*** is that sometimes true love is right next to you. In the movie, Rob and Nita had already spent an entire year in classes together without any attraction to each other. It isn't until they found themselves alone, that they fall in love.

In my opinion, ***Love in Seoul*** was a fantastic movie. It was a sad story, but it taught me the meaning of true love. The characters were genuine and sincere. I liked how Rob and Nita handled being lost. They were strong and trusted each other. In addition, the movie was filled with unforgettable songs. I think that everyone should see this great movie.

Assignment

Using the example from page 116, create a 3 paragraph movie review, of any Korean movie of your choosing.

You will be graded according to the chart below. In addition, there should be no spelling mistakes. All spelling mistakes will result in an automatic 5 point deduction from your grade.

Followed the correct layout	/5
Wrote a well written first paragraph in accordance with pg. 111	/5
Wrote a well written second paragraph in accordance with pg. 112	/5
Wrote a well written third paragraph in accordance with pg. 113	/5
Used apostrophes to show possession correctly	/5
Italicized all movies titles within the paragraphs	/5
Total Score	/30

Assignment Layout

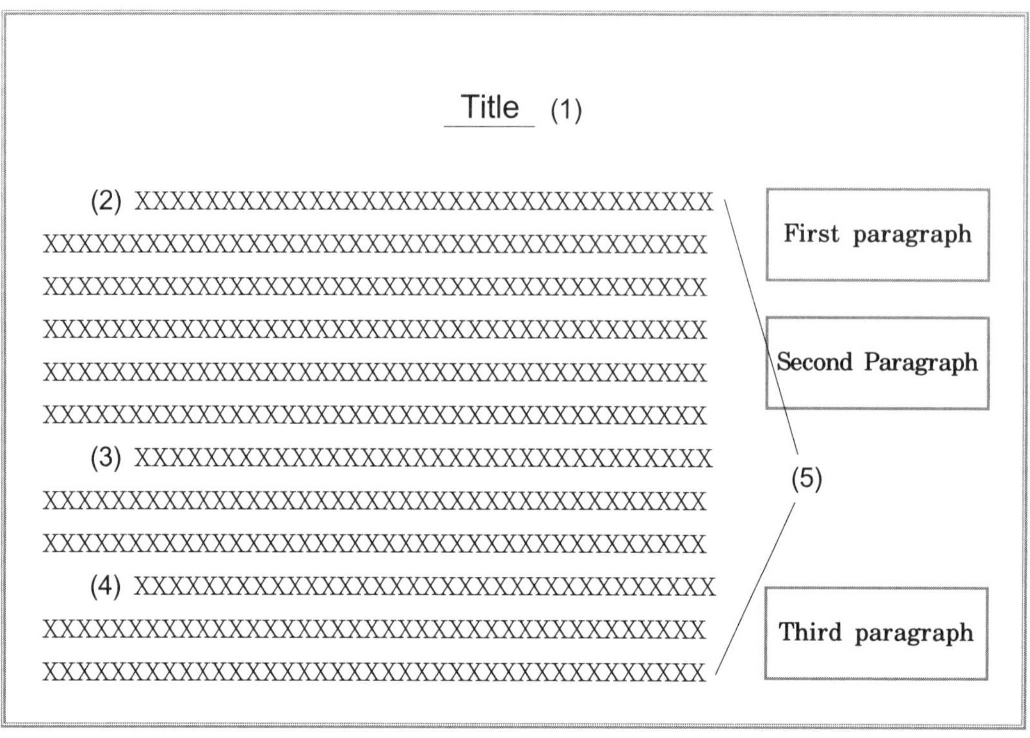

1. Your title should be in the center of your page, underlined, and capitalized correctly.

2.−4. The first sentence of each paragraph should be indented. For the correct way to write each of the three paragraphs, please follow pgs. 110−113.

5. The remaining sentences in your body should align on the right side of your page evenly. There should be two spaces between each line in your composition.

Self–Check List

1. Use the check-list below to make sure you have completed the assignment correctly.

Did you...	Yes	No
follow the correct layout?		
write a well–written first paragraph in accordance with pg. 111?		
write a well–written second paragraph in accordance with pg. 112?		
write a well written third paragraph in accordance with pg. 113?		
write apostrophes to show possession correctly?		
italicize all movies titles within the paragraphs?		
make any spelling mistakes?		

Peer Review

1. Read your partner's assignment. Did your partner write a well written first paragraph? Where does your partner's movie take place? Who are the main characters? Briefly, write the answers below.

2. Read your partner's second paragraph. Did your partner write the main message of the movie? Please write it below.

3. Read your partner's third paragraph. Did your partner recommend this movie to others? Please write your partners recommendation below.

4. Use the check-list below to make sure you partner has completed the assignment correctly.

Did your partner...	Yes	No
follow the correct layout?		
write a well-written first paragraph in accordnace with pg. 111?		
write a well-written second paragraph in accordance with pg. 112?		
write a well-written third paragraph in accordance with pg. 113?		
write apostrophes to show possession correctly?		
italicize all movies titles within the paragraphs?		
make any spelling mistakes?		

5. Discuss your findings and results with your partner.

Review

1. What is an attention getter?

____

____

2. What is an Introductory Paragraph?

____

____

3. What is a Concluding Paragraph?

____

____

4. What are two things that should be found in the first paragraph of a movie review?

a. ______________________________

b. ______________________________

5. What are two things that should be found in the third paragraph of a movie review?

a. ______________________________

b. ______________________________

2. Read the short paragraph below and inserting a, an, and the where needed.

A Great Restaurant

Let me tell you about great restaurant in Sinchon. Name of restaurant is Under the Sea. Under the Sea is famous restaurant, which is located in center of Seoul. Under the Sea has assortment of various fish layed out in buffet style. Buffet at Under the Sea is great. However Under the Sea is most famous for its three ounce king crab burgers. I think that they are the best tasting crab burgers in whole world. . .

3. Read the short paragraph below crossing out any unnecessary sentences.

My Friend Dean

My friend Dean is the hardest working person I know. Just last year Dean bought a new car and broke his arm and ankle, however, he never missed a single day of work. In addition, he even had his wife bring his books to the hospital, so that he could work while he recovered. When Dean was in the hospital if he wasn't working he was watching soccer on tv. Dean really likes to watch tv. Dean also attends classes at a near by university, while most people would have just rested and missed a few classes. Dean on the other hand, despite his broken ankle rode to class on his bike everyday. Dean is a very very hard working person.

4. Which sentence below is grammatically correct?

a. (a) Green tea, unlike beer, is healthy for you.

(b) Green tea unlike beer is healthy for you.

(c) Green tea, unlike beer is healthy for you.

(d) Green tea unlike beer, is healthy for you.

b. (a) Cheetahs are fast on the other hand turtles are slow.

(b) Cheetahs are fast on the other hand, turtles are slow.

(c) Cheetahs are fast, on the other hand turtles are slow.

(d) Cheetahs are fast, on the other hand, turtles are slow.

c. (a) My oldest son is very shy on the other hand my second son is outgoing.

(b) My oldest son is very shy. On the other hand, my second son is outgoing.

(c) My oldest son is very shy, on the other hand my second son is outgoing.

(d) My oldest son is very shy on the other hand, my second son is outgoing.

d. (a) I studied Spanish for over two years, however I can't speak spanish well.

(b) I studied Spanish for over two years however, I can't speak spanish well.

(c) I studied Spanish for over two years however I can't speak spanish well.

(d) I studied Spanish for over two years, however, I can't speak spanish well.

e. (a) I want to buy a new car, however I don't have any money.

(b) I want to buy a new car. However I don't have any money.

(c) I want to buy a new car. However, I don't have any money.

(d) I want to buy a new car however I don't have any money.

f. (a) Whereas professor Smith always tells jokes in class, professor Bright doesn't.

(b) Whereas, professor Smith always tells jokes in class professor Bright doesn't.

(c) Whereas, professor Smith always tells jokes in class, professor Bright doesn't.

(d) Whereas professor Smith always tells jokes in class, professor Bright doesn't.

f. (a) A pillow is very light, while, a table is very heavy.

(b) A pillow is very light, while a table is very heavy.

(c) A pillow is very light while a table is very heavy.

(d) A pillow is very light while, a table is very heavy.

6. Match each word to its correct synonym.

a. warm atmosphere	h. delicious
b. mouth-watering	I. normal
c. affordable	j. creative
d. generic	k. bloody
e. durable	l. long lasting
f. imaginative	m. inexpensive
g. gory	n. friendly atmosphere

Unit 10 It's Delicious!

▶ In this unit, you will learn how to ...

- write food measurements
- use sequence adverbs
- use imperatives
- write a process description composition
- expand your vocabulary while writing

1. Read the composition on the next page. Next, discuss the meanings of any unfamiliar words or phrases, including the bold-faced words and phrases in the composition.

2. Ask your partner if they are a good cook.

3. Ask your partner what they know how to cook.

At the end of this unit, you will be asked to write a four paragraph process description composition on how to make a food of your choice. Each paragraph should be well written following the outline presented in this unit.

An Amazing Grilled Cheese Sandwich

I'm going to teach you how to make an amazing grilled cheese sandwich all by yourself. I can promise your friends and family will love it.

Before we start, you are going to need a few **ingredients**. You will need a two **slices of bread**, once **slice of cheese**, **two strips of bacon**, a **cube of butter**, some potato chips, and one tomato.

First, fry the two slices of bacon in a frying pan, until they are **crisp**. Second, slice the tomato. Third, place the cooked bacon, cheese slice, and two slices of tomato in between the two slices of bread. Then place the butter cube in a clean frying pan and **let it melt**. Next, place the sandwich in the frying pan and **toast it lightly** on both sides. After that, place your sandwich on a plate and add some potato chips. Finally, eat and enjoy.

Now that you know how to make this delicious sandwich, share its great taste with all of your friends and family. Their stomachs will all thank you for it.

LESSON 1 WRITING FOCUS: PRE-WRITING AND BRAINSTORMING

1. Try to think of some of your favorite foods and write them below.

Favorite Foods
Lasagna,

2. Using the list above, choose one food that you feel you can cook well. Write the name of the food you chose on the line below.

____

3. Using the food you wrote down for question number two, use the example below to make your own food recipe.

Strawberry Milkshake Recipe

1/2 cup of strawberries

4 scoops of vanilla ice cream

1 cup of milk

____

____

____

____

____

____

LESSON 2 LANGUAGE FOCUS: FOOD MEASUREMENTS

Uncountable Noun Foods	Unit of Measure
bread	a loaf of bread
flour	a bag of flour
corn	an ear of corn
lettuce	a head of lettuce
milk	a carton of milk
bacon	a package of bacon
meat	a piece / pound / kilogram of meat
chocolate	a bar of chocolate
honey	a jar of honey
soda	a can of soda
water	a bottle of water
cheese	a block / a cube / a pound of cheese
spaghetti	a package of spaghetti
potato chips	a bag of potato chips

LESSON 3 LANGUAGE FOCUS: USING SEQUENCE ADVERBS

One way that we can make a composition flow is by using sequence adverbs. Sequence adverbs are usually used in the order given below.

1. First,
2. Then (Then is the only sequence adverb that is not followed by a comma.)
3. Next,
4. After that,
5. Finally,

Note After first, second, third, etc. can also be used.

ex. ***First***, slice one onion. ***Second***, dice two potatoes. **Then** place the onions and potatoes into the water.

1. Using the words **first**, **second**, **third**, **then**, **next**, and **finally**, place the sentences below in the correct order.

Making a peanut butter and jelly sandwich.

A: Hi __________, what are you doing?
B: I'm trying to make a peanut butter and jelly sandwich, but I don't know how. Would you please help me?
A: Sure, no problem, it's easy.

________ you need two pieces of bread.
________ you need some peanut butter and some jelly.
I like grape jelly, but it's up to you.
________ you need a knife.
________ using the knife spread some peanut butter on one piece of bread.
________ spread some jelly on the other piece of bread.
________ put the pieces of bread together.
________ eat and enjoy!

Unit 10

LESSON 4 VOCABULARY FOCUS

Describing food: Match the verbs with the correct definition

made with	roast	baked
range of	stuffed with	served with
pickled	marinate	seasoned

a. To cook something in an oven ______________________.

b. The list of ingredients in a dish ______________________.

c. Food given with a main dish ______________________.

d. To fill something with food ______________________.

e. To cook something over an open fire ______________________.

f. A number of similar things ______________________.

g. To add spices to a food ______________________.

h. To soak something in a sauce______________________.

i. To use salt to keep a food fresh______________________.

Grammar Focus:

Some things can be ***made from*** something and some things can be ***made with*** something.

Example:

Made with:

Kimchee is made with salt and red pepper paste.
Crab cakes are made with bread and mayonnaise.

Made from:

Rice cakes are made from rice.
Bread is made from wheat.

LESSON 5 LANGUAGE FOCUS: USING IMPERATIVES

1. Match each letter with its correct counterpart to form an imperative sentence.

a. Cut the	m. soy sauce and wasabi together.
b. Spread the	n. ketchup onto the egg.
c. Peel the	o. french fries on the plate.
d. Slice the	p. salt onto the potatoes.
e. Blend the	q. garlic into tiny pieces.
f. Crush the	r. the banana in with the milk.
g. Sprinkle some	s. the cucumber into tiny slivers.
h. Place some	t. apple.
i. Stir the	u. peanut butter on the bread.
j. Mix the	v. chicken into small pieces.
k. Rinse the	w. the soup counter clockwise.
l. Squirt some	x. the lettuce before you put it into the bowel.

2. Use the given words below to make your own unique sentences.

a. (Cut the)

____

b. (Slice the)

____

c. (Sprinkle some)

____

d. (Place some)

____

e. (Peel the)

____

LESSON 6 ORGANIZATION FOCUS: WRITING A PROCESS DESCRIPTION COOKING COMPOSITION

An Amazing Grilled Cheese Sandwich

I'm going to teach you how to make an amazing grilled cheese sandwich all by yourself. I can promise your friends and family will love it.

> The first paragraph is an introductory paragraph. The purpose of this paragraph is to introduce the reader to the food that you are going to teach them how to make. This should be clearly stated in your topic sentence.

Before we start, you are going to need a few ingredients. You will need a two slices of bread, once slice of cheese, two strips of bacon, a cube of butter, some potato chips, and one tomato.

> The purpose of the second paragraph is to let the reader know what ingredients will be needed for the given food dish.

First, fry the two slices of bacon in a frying pan, until they are crisp. Second, slice the tomato. Third, place the cooked bacon, cheese slice, and two slices of tomato in between the two slices of bread. Then place the butter cube in a clean frying pan and let it melt. Next, place the sandwich in the frying pan and toast it lightly on both sides. After that, place your sandwich on a plate and add some potato chips. Finally, eat and enjoy.

> The purpose of the third paragraph is to give the reader a step-by-step instructional guide on how to prepare the given food dish.

Now that you know how to make this delicious sandwich, share its great taste with all of your friends and family. Their stomachs will all thank you for it.

> The last paragraph is a concluding paragraph, which wraps up your composition.

LESSON 7 VOCABULARY FOCUS

1. Examine the use of each word or phrase underlined below and see if you can guess the meaning. If you are not sure of the meaning, ask a classmate or check your dictionary. Once you have found the meanings of all the words and phrases, create your own sentences with the bold-faced words and phrases.

a. To ***add some flavor***, sprinkle some salt in.

b. Bring the stew to a ***simmer***.

c. I like to ***grate*** some cheese over my pasta.

d. Place the potatoes and carrots into a ***crockpot***.

e. Make sure all of the guests have ***utensils***, so that they can eat.

f. You should set a ***timer*** to make sure the bread doesn't over bake.

g. Place the frying pan on the ***burner***.

h. Make sure you use a ***cutting board*** when you cut the vegetables.

i. Use a ***spatula*** to flip the egg.

a. ______________________________

b. ______________________________

c. ______________________________

d. ______________________________

e. ______________________________

f. ______________________________

g. ______________________________

h. ______________________________

i. ______________________________

LESSON 7 EXAMPLE

A Delicious Strawberry Milkshake

I'm going to teach you how to make a delicious strawberry milkshake all by yourself in the comfort of your own home. I guarantee that your mouth will thank you later.

Introductory Paragraph

Before we start, you are going to need a few ingredients. You will need a half cup of sliced strawberries, four scoops of vanilla ice cream, and one cup of milk.

Ingredients

First, scoop out four scoops of vanilla ice cream and place them in a blender. Second, pour in a cup of milk. Third, slice up a half cup of strawberries. Fourth, put the strawberries in the blender. Next, plug in the blender and blend for about one minute. Finally, pour the mixture into glasses and enjoy.

How to make

Now that you know how to make this delicious strawberry milkshake, share this delicious taste with all of your friends and family. All of their mouths will be very thankful.

Concluding Paragraph

Assignment

Using the example from page 134 create a four paragraph instructional guide on how to make a food of your choosing. You will be graded according to the chart below. In addition, there should be no spelling mistakes. All spelling mistakes will result in an automatic 5 point deduction from your grade.

Followed the correct layout	/5
Wrote a well written first paragraph in accordance with pg.134	/5
Wrote a well written second paragraph in accordance with pg.134	/5
Wrote a well written third paragraph in accordance with pg.134	/5
Wrote a well written fourth paragraph in accordance with pg.134	/5
Used sequence adverbs in conjunction with imperatives	/5
Total Score	/30

Assignment Layout

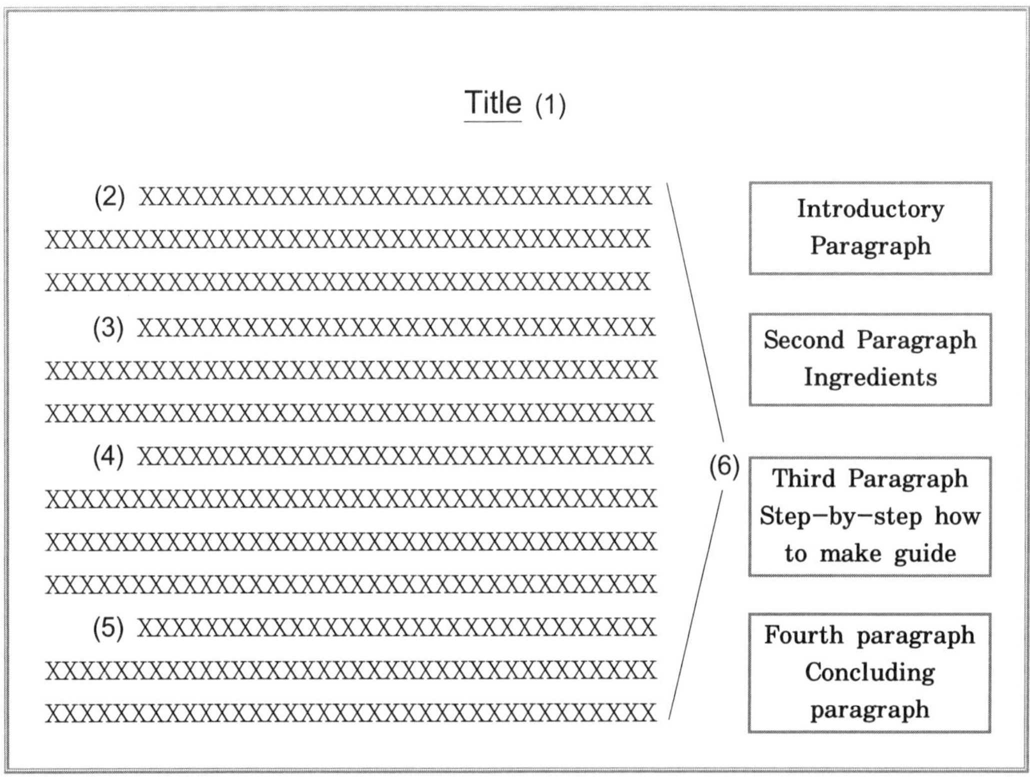

1. Your title should be in the center of your page, underlined, and capitalized correctly.

2.－5. The first sentence of each paragraph should be indented. For the correct way to write each of the three paragraphs, please follow pg. 134.

6. The remaining sentences in your body should align on the right side of your page evenly. There should be two spaces between each line in your composition.

Self-Check List

1. Use the check-list below to make sure you have completed the assignment correctly.

Did you...	Yes	No
follow the correct layout?		
write a well written first paragraph in accordance with pg.134?		
write a well written second paragraph in accordance with pg.134?		
write a well written third paragraph in accordance with pg.134?		
write a well written fourth paragraph in accordance with pg.134?		
use sequence adverbs in conjunction with imperatives?		
make any spelling mistakes?		

Peer Review

1. Read your partner's assignment. Did your partner write a well written first paragraph? Please write the food they will teach us how to prepare below.

2. Read your partner's second paragraph. Write the ingredients that are needed to prepare this food below.

3. Read your partner's third paragraph. Did they use sequence adverbs and imperatives? Write the first and last thing we should do below.

4. Use the check-list below to make sure your partner has completed the assignment correctly.

Did your partner...	Yes	No
follow the correct layout?		
write a well written first paragraph in accordance with pg.134?		
write a well written second paragraph in accordance with pg.134?		
write a well written third paragraph in accordance with pg.134?		
write a well written fourth paragraph in accordance with pg.134?		
use sequence adverbs in conjunction with imperatives?		
make any spelling mistakes?		

5. Discuss your findings and results with your partner.

Writing Flow Unit 11 My Career

▶ In this unit, you will learn how to ...

- write assertively
- write a ***resume***
- address women in a letter
- write a ***cover letter***
- expand your vocabulary when writing

1. Read the cover letter on the next page. Next, discuss the meanings of any unfamiliar words or phrases, including the bold-faced words and phrases in the composition.

2. Discuss with your partner what you think the best and worst jobs are in the world.

3. Discuss with your partner what the three most popular jobs in Korea are.

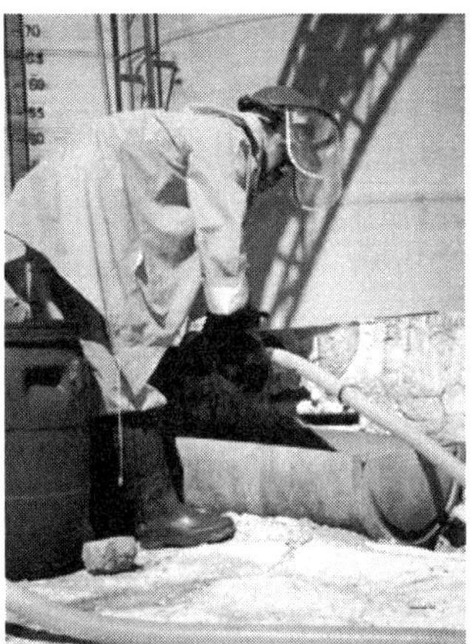

At the end of this unit, you will be asked to write a fictitious cover letter for an imaginary job opening. In your cover letter you must explain why you would be a good candidate for the job in which you are applying. In addition to your composition you must make a resume. Each assignment should be well written following the outline presented in this unit.

Su-Jin Kim
Samsung Apt. Bld. 406 Rm. 303
Myenongil Dong, Gangdong Gu,
Seoul, South Korea 134-808
Tel: (609)-465-9880
Cell: (03)-378-2189
SJ@hanmail.net

March 27, 2010

Mr. Byung Chan Cho
Yi Soon Shin University English Department
San 53-1
Bongchun Dong, Gwanak Gu
Seoul, South Korea 452-503

Dear Mr. Cho,

I am interested in the English professor position which appeared in the Baekjae Ilbo this week. My resume is enclosed for your review. Due to my **related experience** and **excellent capabilities, I would appreciate your consideration** for this job opening. I am sure that I will be an excellent addition to your university.

I recently graduated from the University of Colorado with a master's degree in TESEL / TESOL, where I was ranked first in my class. I know Yi Soon Shin University has a **well respected** teacher training program, and with my education in TESEL / TESOL I feel that I can be a **valuable asset** to your program.

In addition, I am a certified speech trainer with extensive experience in curriculum design. During my time at the University of Colorado I worked as an intern at Rocky Mountain Junior College for two years, while receiving additional experience as a teachers aid my senior year at the University of Colorado.

I look forward to **putting my knowledge and experience into practice at your prestigious university**. I will be away next week on a business trip, but I am free any day the following week for an interview. I can be reached at 609)-465-9880 or (03)-378-2189. Thank you for your consideration, and **I look forward to hearing from you soon**.

Respectfully yours,

Su-Jin Kim

Su-Jin Kim

LESSON 1 PREWRITING AND BRAINSTORMING

1. Please answer each question with a full sentence.

a. In the future what job would you like to have?

b. What are some things that would help you get this job?

c. What have you done to prepare for this job?

LESSON 2 LANGUAGE FOCUS: WRITING ASSERTIVELY

When we write a cover letter, we should use strong assertive language. Using strong assertive language shows you have confidence not only in yourself, but also in your abilities. Both attributes are attractive to perspective employers.

Below each ***sentence starter*** is basically stating the same thing, yet each expression has a slightly different strength connotation to it. The column labled strong is an example of assertive language.

Strong	Weak
I want to	I am thinking about
I would like to	I am considering
I have to	Possibly I could
I must	Maybe I could
I am sure that	Maybe I will
I feel that	I hope I can
I can	I wish to
I will	I might

1. Using the chart above to make each sentence below more assertive.

a. Possibly I could be a good teacher at your school.

____

b. I hope I can be a great flight attendant.

____

c. I might help your company sell more products.

____

d. I should become better with practice.

____

LESSON 3 WRITING FOCUS: RESUME

For a resume you should......

※ Make the most important information easy to see.
※ Keep the language clear and simple.
※ Make sure it is easy to read / not cluttered.
※ List your job and education history in reverse chronological order.
※ Type the resume.
※ Make sure there are no spelling errors.
※ Don't write resume at the top of the page.
※ Keep everything on one page.

John Doe
234 East Lake Ave.
Austin, Texas 21765 USA
(Tel.) (02) 432-7777
(Cell) (010) 434-8799
JD23@yahoo.com

OBJECTIVE

To obtain a position as an university English professor

PROFESSIONAL EXPERIENCE

Gangnam University, Gangnam, South Korea, 2007-present
Responsible for teaching English as a second language to university students. Preparing lesson plans, as well as giving exams.

Beijing University, Suxzu, China 2005-2007

Responsible for teaching English as a second language to university students. Preparing lesson plans, as well as giving exams.

EDUCATION

Master of TESL / TESOL, University of Colorado, 2003
Bachelor of English University of Kansas, 2000
Berkwood High School, 1996

SPECIAL SKILLS

Certified speech trainer
Extensive experience in curriculum development

AWARDS

TESL Certificate
Published two books, Winning English 2001, Smart English 2004

LESSON 4 ORGANIZATION FOCUS: LAYING OUT A RESUME

(1) John Doe
234 East Lake Ave.
Austin, Texas 21765 USA
(Tel.) (02) 432-7777
(Cell) (010) 434-8799
JD23@yahoo.com

(1)

On a resume your name and contact information are usually placed at the top of your page and centered. This information can be written in bold-faced type, however, don't try to make it look to fancy. Your contact information should be written in the following order:

(English Example)

1. Name in full .... (John Doe)
2. Address .... (234 East Lake Ave.)
3. City, State .... (Austin, Texas)
4. Zip code, Country .... (21765 USA)
5. Phone number .... (02) 432-7777
6. Cell-phone number .... (010) 434-8799
7. E-mail address .... (JD23@yahoo.com)

(Korean Example)

1. Name in full .... (Eun-Me Jung)
2. Address .... (Hyundai Apt. Bld. 302 Rm 702
3. Town, District .... (Cheonho dong, (Gangdong gu)
4. City, Country, Zip code .... (Seoul, South Korea 121-858)
6. Phone number .... ((02)-465-6323)
7. Cell-phone number .... ((010)-378-7732)
8. E-mail address .... (SJ@hanmail.net)

(1)	OBJECTIVE
	To obtain a position as an university English professor

(1)

Your title "OBJECTIVE" should standout from the rest of your text. There are various ways to do this, however, in the example the title has a larger font and is written in full caps. The important thing is not how it is written, as long as it stands out and look neat.

(2)

The purpose of the objective section on your resume is to let the receiver of your resume know exactly which position you are applying for. In the example the fictitious person is applying to be a university English teacher. At an university there are many departments. At any one given time each department could be looking for a new professor. It is important for the author of this resume to specify which department, as well as, job they are applying for.

PROFESSIONAL EXPERIENCE

Gangnam University, Gangnam, South Korea, 2007–present
Responsible for teaching English as a second language to University students. Preparing lesson plans, as well as giving exams.

Beijing University, Suxzu, China 2005–2007
Responsible for teaching English as a second language to University students. Preparing lesson plans, as well as giving exams.

(1)

Under "PROFESSIONAL EXPERIENCE" you should list own jobs that you have had that are relevant to the job you are applying for.

(2)

For example this person would like to be an university English professor, therefore previous jobs in which he taught English would best fit this resume. If this man had previously worked at a movie theater it would have little relevance for this resume as working at a movie theater does not in anyway relate to teaching English.

(3)

On a resume you must list the jobs you had in reverse chronological order, ending with your most recent job. If you are still at that job, you should use the date you started followed by a dash and ending with the word "present", to signify that you are still currently working at that place.

EDUCATION

Master of TESL / TESOL, University of Colorado, 2003
Bachelor of English University of Kansas, 2000
Berkwood High School, 1996

(1)

Under "EDUCATION" you must list the schools you have attended in reverse chronological order starting with your highest degree of completion and ending with the high school you graduated from.

(2)

For your education you only need to list the years you graduated.

(1)

SPECIAL SKILLS
Certified speech trainer Extensive experience in curriculum development

(1)

The "SPECIAL SKILLS" section of your resume is where you list any skills you have acquired which would set you apart from other applicants and or further qualify you for the position you are applying for. In the example above the fictitious applicant has had extensive experience in curriculum development, in addition to being certified in speech training. Both of these are very desirable skills for English professors to have, possibly making this applicant more desirable to the university in which he is applying.

(1)

AWARDS
TESL Certificate Published two books, Winning English 2001, Smart English 2004

(1)

The "AWARDS" section of your resume is where you list any awards you have acquired which would set you apart from other applicants and or further qualify you for the position you are applying for. In the example above the fictitious applicant was has received a TESL certificate, in addition to publishing two books. Both of these things could possibly make this applicant better qualified for the job he is applying for.

LESSON 5 LANGUAGE FOCUS: ADDRESSING WOMEN IN BUSINESS LETTERS

When addressing women in letters there are several titles you can use, however, it is very important to choose the correct title, or you may offend the women receiving your letter.

Mrs. = is used for a women who is or has been married.

Miss = is used for a women who is not married.

Ms. = can be used for a married or unmarried women.

Note all titles have a period proceeding them, except Miss, where a period is not needed.

Unit 11

LESSON 5 WRITING FOCUS: WRITING A COVER LETTER

Section 1 : Your contact information and date

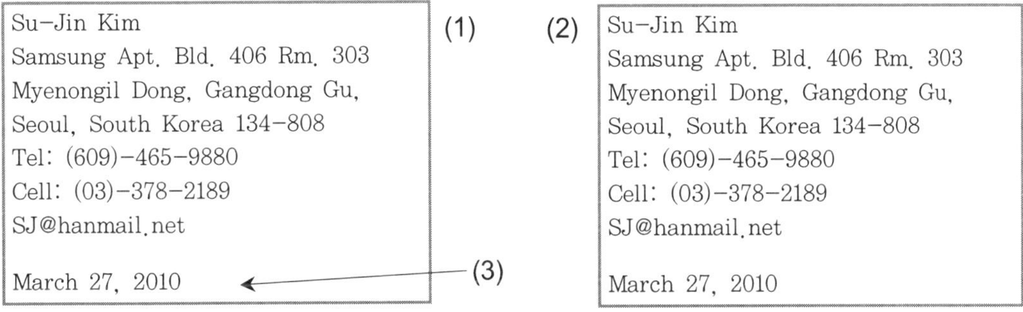

(1)

Su-Jin Kim
Samsung Apt. Bld. 406 Rm. 303
Myenongil Dong, Gangdong Gu,
Seoul, South Korea 134-808
Tel: (609)-465-9880
Cell: (03)-378-2189
SJ@hanmail.net

March 27, 2010 ← (3)

(2)

Su-Jin Kim
Samsung Apt. Bld. 406 Rm. 303
Myenongil Dong, Gangdong Gu,
Seoul, South Korea 134-808
Tel: (609)-465-9880
Cell: (03)-378-2189
SJ@hanmail.net

March 27, 2010

(1) The first section of a cover letter should contain your contact information. Your contact information can be placed either at the top far left corner of your paper or in the top center (2). This choice is purely personal and has no effect on the quality of your letter. Your contact information should be ordered as follows:

(English Example)

1. Name in full ·· (Sam Dell)
2. Address ·· (589 West Bay Ave.)
3. City, State ·· (Goshen, New Jersey)
4. Zip code, Country ·· (90632 USA)
5. Phone number ·· (609) 522-0560
6. Cell-phone number ·· (602) 729-2288
7. E-mail address ·· (SD@yahoo.com)

(Korean Example)

1. Name in full ·· (Su-Jin Park)
2. Address ·· (Samsung Apt. Bld. 406 Rm 303
3. Town, District ·· (Myeongil dong, (Gangdong gu)
4. City, Country, Zip code ·· (Seoul, South Korea 134-808)
6. Phone number ·· ((609)-465-9880)
7. Cell-phone number ·· ((010)-378-2189)
8. E-mail address ·· (SJ@hanmail.net)

(3) The date in which you have sent your cover letter should follow your contact information. The date should appear in this order: **First Month, Second Day, Third Year.**

Section 2: Employer's contact information and greeting / salutation

(1)

Mr. Byung Chan Cho
Yi Soon Shin University English Department
San 53-1
Bongchun Dong, Gwanak Gu
Seoul, South Korea 452-503

Dear Mr. Cho, ← (2)

(1)

The second section of your cover letter is the employer's contact information. In some cases you may not have the employer's contact information, and in that case it is ok to omit this section from your cover letter. If you have this information, however, it should be written in to your cover letter following the same order as your contact information.

(2)

After the employer's contact information comes the greeting / salutation. Many greetings and salutations exist in English, however, for cover letters "Dear" is best. Depending if you are contacting a man or a women "Dear" should be followed by Mr., Ms., Miss., or Mrs. and the person's last name. In cases where you don't know the contact person's name write "To whom it may concern", "Dear Sir/Madam", or "Dear Reader" (3). In all cases your greeting / salutation should be followed by a comma.

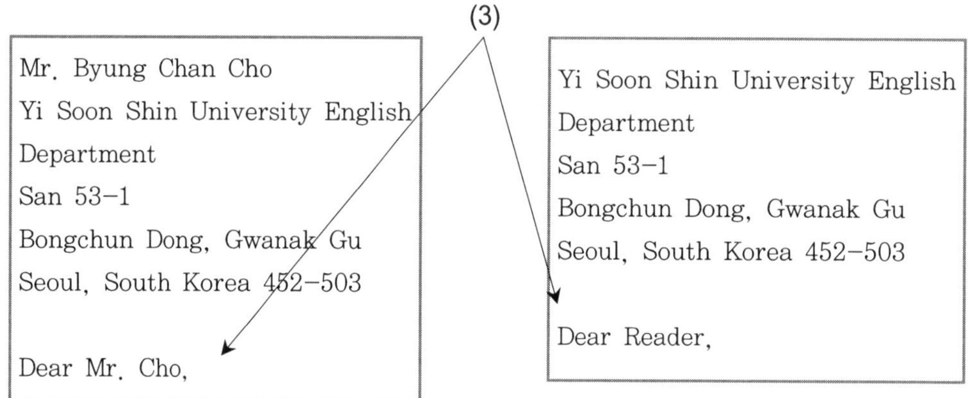

(3)

Mr. Byung Chan Cho
Yi Soon Shin University English Department
San 53-1
Bongchun Dong, Gwanak Gu
Seoul, South Korea 452-503

Dear Mr. Cho,

Yi Soon Shin University English Department
San 53-1
Bongchun Dong, Gwanak Gu
Seoul, South Korea 452-503

Dear Reader,

Section 3: The first paragraph

(1)

> I am interested in the English professor position which appeared in the Baekjae Ilbo this week. My resume is enclosed for your review. Due to my related experience and excellent capabilities, I would appreciate your consideration for this job opening. I am sure that I will be an excellent addition to your university.

(1)

The first paragraph of your cover letter should include information on why you have written this letter. It should also mention the job in which you are applying and where you found the job listing.

Section 4: The middle paragraph(s)

(2)

> I recently (3) graduated from the University of Colorado with a master's degree in TESEL / TESOL, where (4) I was ranked first in my class. I know Yi Soon Shin University has a well respected teacher training program, and with my education in TESEL / TESOL I feel that I can be a valuable asset to your program.
>
> In addition, (3) I am a certified speech trainer with extensive experience in curriculum design. During my time at the University of Colorado (4) I worked as an intern at Rocky Mountain Junior College for two years, while receiving additional experience as a teachers aid my senior year at the University of Colorado.

(2)

The middle paragraph(s) of your cover letter should include specific information as to how you and your qualifications match the job you are applying for. Support for your qualifications should come from your resume. However keep in mind that you are only referencing your resume, not rewriting it (3). In addition, this section of your paper should highlight important qualifications and benefits that you could bring to the job you are applying, yet were unable to write in your resume (4).

Section 5: The final paragraph

(1)

> I look forward to putting my knowledge and experience into practice at your prestigious university. I will be away next week on a business trip, but I am free any day the following week for an interview. I can be reached at 609)-465-9880 or (03)-378-2189. Thank you for your consideration, and I look forward to hearing from you soon.

(1)

In the final paragraph of your cover letter respectfully bring your letter to a close. In this section you should once again mention your sincere interest in the job, as well as, where and when you can be contacted. End your letter by thanking the recipient for their time and effort.

Section 6: The complimentary closing and signature

(1)

> Respectfully yours,
>
> *Su-Jin Kim*
>
> Su-Jin Kim

(1)

The last part of your cover letter is your complimentary closing and signature. For a formal letter there are only a few complimentary closings that you should use. A few acceptable complimentary closings include:

- Sincerely,
- Respectfully yours,
- Thank you for your time and consideration,
- Thank you,

(note all complimentary closings are followed by a comma)

Your complimentary closing should be followed by one space and then a handwritten signature. Your handwritten signature should be followed by one space and then your full name typed below. In a block style letter your closing should be placed at the bottom left hand side of your page even with your other paragraphs.

LESSON 6 VOCABULARY FOCUS

1. Examine the use of each word or phrase underlined below and see if you can guess the meaning. If you are not sure of the meaning, ask a classmate or check your dictionary. Once you have found the meanings of all the words and phrases, create your own sentences with the bold-faced words and phrases.

a. I graduated **with honors** from my university.

b. I obtained an **associates degree** from DCC College.

c. I am a very **punctual** person.

d. I work well **under pressure**.

e. You don't have to worry about training me, as **I catch on quick**.

f. I am very good at **collaborating** with others.

g. I have a **knack for** design.

h. I can provide several **reputable** references.

i. I would like to know a little bit more about **what the job entails**.

a. ______________________________

b. ______________________________

c. ______________________________

d. ______________________________

e. ______________________________

f. ______________________________

g. ______________________________

h. ______________________________

i. ______________________________

LESSON 7 EXAMPLE

Gabriell Mattera
765 Pinewood Ave.
Belmont, Pennsylvania 34576 USA
Tel: (609)-465-9780
Cell: (03)-378-2159
Gab@yahoo.com

April 23, 2010

Mr. Richard Bell
Southern Airlines
23 Blackberry Drive
Clearwater, Florida 99765 USA

Dear Mr. Bell,

I am interested in the flight attendant position which appeared on your web site. My outgoing personality and my strong desire to be a flight attendant make me an excellent candidate for your company.

I recently graduated from Temple University with a four year bachelor's degree in tourism, where I was ranked first in my class.

Although a recent graduate, I am well prepared to be a great flight attendant. At my university I received training in customer care and emergency services. In addition to these skills, I am fluent in Japanese, English, and Chinese.

I look forward to putting my skills and knowledge into practice on your acclaimed airline. I have enclosed my resume for your review. I am free any day next week for an interview. I can be reached at 609)-465-9780 or (03)-378-2159. If I haven't heard from you by next week, I will call you to schedule an interview. Thank you for your consideration, and I look forward to hearing from you soon.

Respectfully yours,

Gabriell Mattera

Gabriell Mattera

Assignment

Using the example from page 156 you have to write a cover letter for a fictions job ad to which you are applying. In addition to your cover letter, you must also write a resume to accompany it. Your resume should follow the layout presented on pgs.145–149. You will be graded according to the chart below. In addition there should be no spelling mistakes. All spelling mistakes will result in an automatic 5 point deduction from your grade.

Followed the correct layout for both assignments	/6
Wrote a well written resume in accordance with pgs. 145–149	/6
Wrote a well written cover letter in accordance with pgs. 151–154	/6
Wrote relevant information connecting both your resume and cover letter	/6
Wrote assertively	/6
Total Score	/30

Assignment Layout

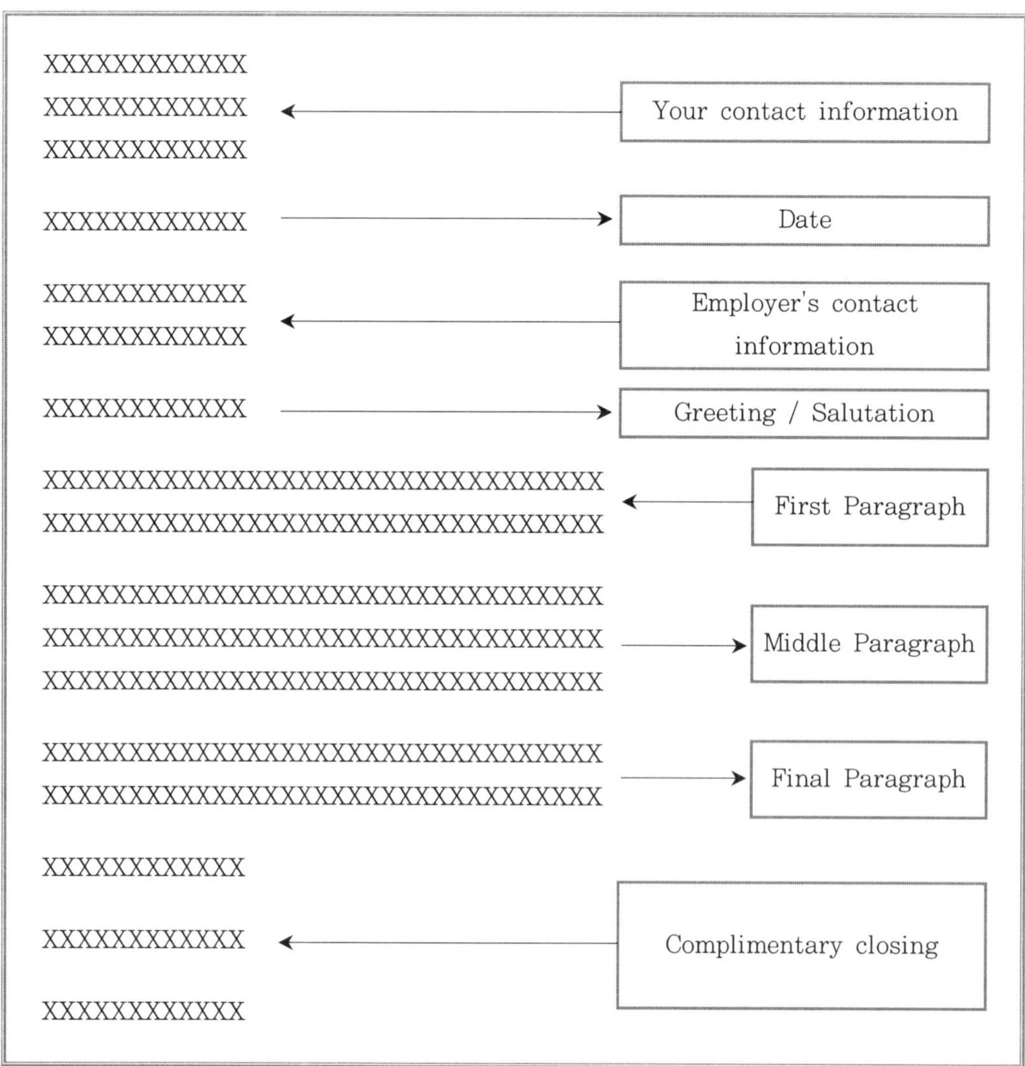

- Make sure all sections of your cover letter align on the left side of your page.
- Furthermore, be sure to keep your cover letter to no more than one page.
- The lines for this type of letter should be single not double spaced.

Self-Check List

1. Use the check-list below to make sure you have completed the assignment correctly.

Did you...	Yes	No
follow the correct layout?		
write a well written resume in accordance with pgs. 145–149?		
Write a well written cover letter in accordance with pgs. 151–154?		
Write relevant information connecting both your resume and cover letter?		
write assertively		
make any spelling mistakes?		

Peer Review

1. Read your partner's cover letter. Write the name of the company your partner is applying to. Next, write the type of job that they are applying to.

2. Read your partner's cover letter. Write two reasons why your partner feels they are qualified for the job to which they are applying?

3. Read your partner's cover letter. Write when your partner is available for an interview below.

4. Use the check-list below to make sure your partner has completed the assignment correctly.

Did your partner...	Yes	No
follow the correct layout?		
write a well written resume in accordance with pgs. 145-149?		
Write a well written cover letter in accordance with pgs. 151-154?		
Write relevant information connecting both your resume and cover letter?		
write assertively		
make any spelling mistakes?		

5. Discuss your findings and results with your partner.

Unit 12 I Have a Complaint

▶ **In this unit, you will learn how to ...**

- use *in*, *at*, and *on* when writing
- use ***would you*** and ***could you*** to make polite requests.
- write a modified block style complaint letter
- address an envelope
- expand your vocabulary when writing

1. Read the complaint letter on the next page. Next, discuss the meanings of any unfamiliar words or phrases, including the bold-faced words and phrases in the composition.

2. Try to think of some different reasons that you might want to complain to a company, restaurant, school, etc.

   1. ______________________________
   2. ______________________________
   3. ______________________________
   4. ______________________________

3. Discuss with your partner what you would do in each of the situations below? Write your answers below.

   1. You bought a printer for ₩100,000, but when you got your credit card bill they charged you ₩500,000.

      ____

      ____

   2. You ordered a jacket online and they sent you a skirt instead.

      ____

      ____

At the end of this unit, you will be asked to write a fictitious complaint letter. In your letter you must explain why you are complaining and how you would like to be compensated for your problem(s). In addition you must address an envelope to accompany your letter. Each assignment should be well written following the outline presented in this unit.

Daniel Boone
765 Seagull Ave.
Buckhannon, WV 34576
USA
Tel: (609)-465-9780
Cell: (103)-378-2159
DB44@yahoo.com

April 23, 2010

Ms. Angela Hernandez
KES Electronic Company
35 Harvest Drive
Blackwater, Kentucky 99765 USA

Dear Ms. Hernandez:

Re: Order No. 12345

On Saturday April 10th 2010, I ordered an KES Mini Blast Mp3 Player model no. 5487 from your website www.KES.com.

Unfortunately, I have had several problems with this mp3 player. First, I have been unable to use my Mini Blast Mp3 Player in my 2009 Eagle SUV. Whenever I try to connect my Mini Blast Mp3 Player, the player reads **uncompatible device**, however, on your website it says that the KES Mini Blast Mp3 Player is compatible with ever car radio **manufactured** after 2007.

Secondly, the KES Mini Blast Mp3 Player was **advertised** on your website as being able to hold three thousand songs, but my Mini Blast Mp3 Player says that its memory is full after **uploading** just one thousand five hundred songs.

To resolve this problem, I would like your company to fully **reimburse** me for this product.

I look forward to your reply and **resolution** to my problem. Please contact me at the above email or call me at home (609)-465-9780 anytime after 5p.m. If I have not heard from you by the end of next week, I will **pursue legal actions**.

Thank you,

Daniel Boone

Daniel Boone

enc. Credit Card Receipt

LESSON 1 LANGUAGE FOCUS: USING IN, AT, AND ON

The uses for *in*, *at*, and *on* can be broken up into two categories, uses for location and uses for time.

Rules for ***location*** are as follows:

Using in

1. *In* is used for locations inside areas such as cities, parts of cities, countries, continents, regions, deserts, valleys, as well as with, words like region, area, and zone.

Ex.

Manhattan is located *in* New York City.
There are many ancient temples *in* Asia.

2. *In* is used for areas within a three dimensional space, such as a building, elevator, magazine, book, cup, pocket etc.

Ex.

I met her *in* the elevator.
I saw his picture *in* a magazine.

3. *In* is use for vehicles which don't permit much movement.

Ex.

I have four people *in* my car.
Have you ever ridden *in* a hot air balloon?

Using at

1. *__At__* is used for places on a map which are not considered to be dimensional. In this situation at is used thought to simply be a location.

Ex.

Let's meet *__at__* the park.
I have to stop *__at__* the store and pick up some milk.

2. *__At__* is used to describe being outside or in the vicinity of a building or place, but not in it.

Ex.

I left my car *__at__* the school.
I bought this *__at__* Gwanghamoon station.

3. *__At__* is also used with objects such as doors, windows, blackboards, and desks to show that a person is interacting with the object mentioned.

Ex.

Somebody is *__at__* the door.
Look *__at__* the blackboard.

Using on

1. ***On*** is used to show contact with a line or surface such as a ceiling roof, floor, river, lake, desk, window, counter, chair, etc.

Ex.

There is a mosquito ***on*** the wall.
Put the cup ***on*** the counter.

2. ***On*** is used for animals used for human transportation such as camels, horses, donkeys, etc.

Ex.

In the past, people rode ***on*** horses to go places.
When I went to Egypt, I rode ***on*** a camel.

3. ***On*** is also used with vehicles which permit freedom of movement such as boats, big airplanes, bicycle, bus, train, etc.

Ex.

Several times, while I was ***on*** the plane I got up to stretch.
I hate riding ***on*** crowded trains and buses.

Confusing Location uses for in, at, on

1. He is ***at*** the hospital ······································ man is visiting the hospital)
   He is ***in*** the hospital ························ (The man is a patient in the hospital)

2. She is ***in*** her house ·······························(The woman is inside of her home)
   She is ***at*** home ············· (Home is simply a point at which the woman is)

3. Vicky is ***at*** the beach ····················· (a location somewhere near the beach)
   Vicky is ***on*** the beach ··············· (actually standing or lying on the sand)

4. Ben sat ***at*** his desk ·························· (a location near the desk in a chair)
   Ben sat ***on*** his desk ································ (on the top surface of the desk)

5. The boats were floating ***on*** the lake ························· (The water's surface)
   The fish were ***in*** the lake ································· (viewing lake as container)

Rules for ***time*** are as follows:

Using in

1. ***In*** is used for periods of time such as centuries, years, seasons, months, and parts of the day.

Ex.

In the 1400's people didn't have electricity.
I always exercise ***in*** the morning.

1. ***In*** is used to show that there was enough time.

Ex.

They arrived ***in*** time to catch the last train.
The made it to the play ***in*** time to see the opening act.

Using at

1. ***At*** is used for a point in time,

Ex.

Lets meet ***at*** 5 o' clock.
We talked about it ***at*** lunch.

2. ***At*** is used to refer to holiday seasons. (not the day)

Ex.

People are always more happy ***at*** Christmas.
Churches are usually most busy ***at*** Easter.

3. ***At*** is used with ages in relation to time.

Ex.

He died ***at*** the age of twenty.
He became a doctor ***at*** the age of eighty.

Using on

1. *On* is used for days.

   Ex.

I have to go to work ***on*** Monday.
What are you going to do ***on*** Thanksgiving?

2. *On* is used to refer to a person's arrival at a scheduled time.

   Ex.

Make sure you are ***on*** time for your interview.
We arrived ***on*** time.

1. Use the rules you have learned about *in*, *at*, and *on* to complete the paragraph below.

A Day in the Life of John

John wakes up (a)_____ six o' clock (b)______ the morning everyday. (c) ______ the morning John likes to exercise (d)_____ the park before going to work. John works (e)_____ DEP Bank. He has (f)______ be (g)_____ work by nine o' clock, or his boss gets very angry. John doesn't like when his boss is angry, so he always arrives (h)______ time. To make it to work (i)______ time John takes the subway. (j)_______ the subway, John likes (k)______ read the newspaper. John thinks that there is a lot of important information that people need to know (l)______ the newspaper. Once John arrives (m)_______ work he goes straight into his office. Once John is (n)_______ his office he puts his hat and coat (o)______ a hook (p)______ the wall and then he sits (q)_______ his desk and checks his email. After John checks his email, he looks (r)_______ any papers that have been left (s)______ his desk by his secretary. After work John likes to stop (t)_______ Starbean Coffee Shop and drink a cup of coffee. Once John arrives home he eats dinner and then he sits (u)______ his living room (v)_____ his couch and watches tv.

LESSON 2 LANGUAGE FOCUS: USING WOULD YOU AND COULD YOU TO MAKE REQUESTS

To make polite requests we can use ***would you*** and ***could you***.

Polite requests:
I ***would like*** my money refunded.
Could you please replace my broken phone?
Impolite requests:
I want my money refunded.
Can you replace my broken phone?

1. Using the examples above, try to change each impolite request into a polite request.

a. Can you let me know by next Monday?

____

b. Check your account.

____

c. I want your company to send somebody to fix it.

____

d. Can you credit my account?

____

e. Look into these matters.

____

f. I want you to send me the updated information.

____

LESSON 3 WRITING FOCUS: WRITING A MODIFIED BLOCK COMPLAINT LETTER

Section 1: YOUR CONTACT INFORMATION AND DATE

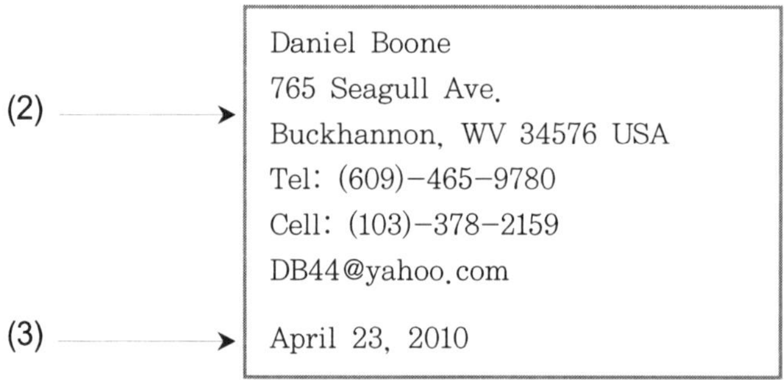

(2) → Daniel Boone
765 Seagull Ave.
Buckhannon, WV 34576 USA
Tel: (609)-465-9780
Cell: (103)-378-2159
DB44@yahoo.com

(3) → April 23, 2010

(1)

The first section of a modified block complaint letter is your contact information. Your contact information is placed at the top far right corner of your paper. The let edge of your contact information should align evenly(2). Your contact information should be ordered as follows:

(English Example)

1. Name in Full .... (Paul King)
2. Address .... (389 East Sky Ave.)
3. City, State .... (Ford, New York)
4. Zip code, Country .... (08218 USA)
5. Phone number .... (302) 543-0960
6. Cell-phone number .... (870) 209-2118
7. E-mail address .... (PK2@yahoo.com)

(Korean Example)

1. Name in full .... (Ki-Hyun Do)
2. Address .... (Samsung Apt. Bld. 506 Rm 803
3. Town, District .... (Mia dong, Seongbuk gu)
4. City, Country, Zip code .... (Seoul, South Korea 123-678)
6. Phone number .... ((809)-564-9820)
7. Cell-phone number .... ((011)-378-2559)
8. E-mail address .... (Do@hotmail.net)

(3)

The date in which you have sent your complaint letter should follow your contact information. The date should appear in this order: Frist Month, Second Day, Third Year.

Section 2:

THE RECEIVING PARTY'S CONTACT INFORMATION AND REASON FOR LETTER

(1) Ms. Angela Hernandez
KES Electronic Company
35 Harvest Drive
Blackwater, Kentucky 99765 USA

Dear Ms. Hernandez:

(4) → Re: Order No. 12345

(1)

The second section of your complaint letter is the company's, business', person's etc. contact information. It should be written in to your cover letter following the same order as your contact information.

(2)

After the employer's contact information comes the greeting / salutation. Many greetings and salutations exist in English, however, for complaint and business letters "Dear" is best. Depending if you are contacting a man or a women "Dear" should be followed by Mr., Ms., Miss., or Mrs. and the person's last name. In cases where you don't know the contact person's name you should try to at least put their title. Never use Dear Sir/Madam etc. (3). For a complaint letter, in all cases your greeting / salutation should be followed by two semicolons.

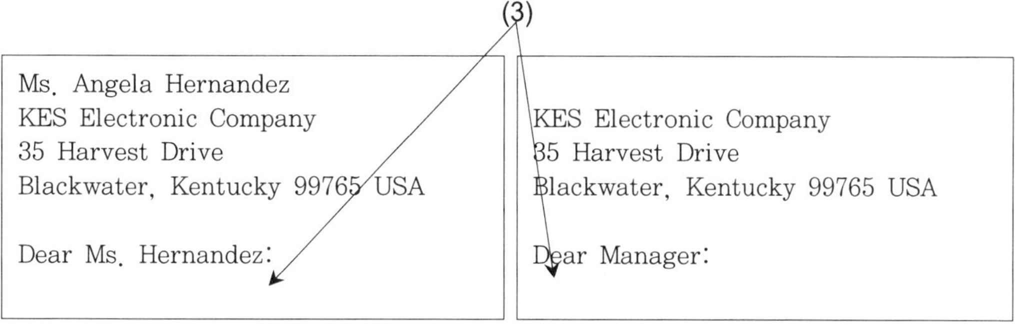
(3)

Ms. Angela Hernandez
KES Electronic Company
35 Harvest Drive
Blackwater, Kentucky 99765 USA

Dear Ms. Hernandez:

KES Electronic Company
35 Harvest Drive
Blackwater, Kentucky 99765 USA

Dear Manager:

(4)

In some cases when writing a complaint letter your may follow your greeting / salutation with the abbreviation "Re.". "Re." stands for reason and lets your reader know why you have written your letter. In most cases "Re" is followed by a model or serial number of a product or shipment.

Section 3: THE FIRST PARAGRAPH

(1)

(2) On Saturday April 10th 2010, (3) I ordered an KES Mini Blast mp3 player model no. 5487 (4) from your website www.KES.com.

(1)

The fist paragraph of your complaint letter should give the date and time of when you purchased something or when a certain problem occurred (2). Next, your paragraph should give the product name with serial or model number if available (3). If you are not writing to complain about a product at this point you state the problem which occurred. This should be followed by the location at which the problem occurred (4).

Section 4: THE MIDDLE PARAGRAPH(S)

Unfortunately, I have had several problems with this mp3 player. First, (2) I have been unable to use my Mini Blast mp3 player in my 2009 Eagle SUV. Whenever I try to connect my Mini Blast mp3 player the player reads uncompatible device, however, on your website it says that the KES Mini Blast mp3 player is compatible with ever car radio manufactured after 2007.

Secondly, the KES Mini Blast mp3 player was **advertised** on your website as being able to hold three thousand songs, but my Mini Blast mp3 player says that its memory is full after **uploading** just one thousand five hundred songs.

(1)

The second and third paragraph of your complaint letter should state what the problem(s) was/were that has caused you to write this letter (2). You should try to be as specific as possible explaining your with details letting the reader understand the situation as clearly as possible.

Note Multiple middle paragraphs are not always needed in complaint letters. If you have only one problem, then one paragraph is sufficient.

Section 5: THE RESOLUTION PARAGRAPH

To resolve this problem, I would like your company to fully reimburse me for this product.

(1)

The resolution paragraph states how you would like to see the mentioned problem resolved.

Section 6: THE CONCLUDING PARAGRAPH

I look forward to your reply and resolution to my problem. (2) Please contact me at the above email or call me at home (609)-465-9780 anytime after 5p.m. (3) If I have not heard from you by the end of next week, (4) I will pursue legal actions.

(1)

The concluding paragraph of your complaint letter restates your contact information and availability (2), in addition to setting a time limit for the mentioned problem to be resolved (3). In some cases, but not in all, depending on how strong you want to be an ultimatum can be written into this paragraph (4).

Section 7: THE CLOSING

(1)

Thank you,
Daniel Boone
Daniel Boone

(1)

The last part of your complaint letter is your complimentary closing and signature. For a formal letter there are only a few complimentary closings that you should use. A few acceptable complimentary closings include:

- Sincerely,
- Respectfully yours,
- Thank you for your time and consideration,
- Thank you,

(note all complimentary closings are followed by a comma)

Your complimentary closing should be followed by one space and then a handwritten signature. Your handwritten signature should be followed by one space and then your full name typed below. For a modified block letter your closing should align on the right side of your page under your contact information.

Section 8: INCLUDED ITEMS

(1)

enc. Credit Card Receipt

(1)

In some cases after your complimentary closing you may mention that you have enclosed something in the letter. For example possible a receipt, warranty, picture etc. This should be labeled "enc," and appear at the bottom left hand corner of your letter.

(2)

c. Attorney K. Brown

cc. Professor S. Kim, Professor J. Hur

(2)

Additionally, after your complimentary closing you might want to mention to the reader that you have sent a copy of this letter to someone or several other people to read. This is done by writing "c." for one person or "cc." for multiple people followed by their names.

LESSON 4 WRITING FOCUS: ADDRESSING A LETTER

(1) Daniel Boone
765 Seagull Ave.
Buckhannon, WV 34576 USA

STAMP

(2) Ms. Angela Hernandez
KES Electronic Company
35 Harvest Drive
Blackwater, Kentucky 99765 USA

(1)

When addressing an envelope place your contact information in the far top left hand corner of the envelope. Your contact information should be listed in this order:

(English Example)

1. Name in Full ………… (Daniel Boone)
2. Address ………… (765 Seagull Ave.)
3. City, State ………… (Buckhannon, WV)
4. Zip code, Country ………… (34576 USA)

(Korean Example)

1. Name in full ………… (Ki–Hyun Do)
2. Address ………… (Samsung Apt. Bld. 506 Rm 803
3. Town, District ………… (Mia dong, Seongbuk gu)
4. City, Country, Zip code ………… (Seoul, South Korea 123–678)

(2)

When addressing an envelope place the receiver's contact information in the center of the envelope. The receiver's contact information should be listed in the same order as your contact information.

Note When addressing an envelope you don't put telephone numbers, cell-phone numbers or email addresses.

LESSON 5 VOCABULARY FOCUS

1. Examine the use of each word or phrase underlined below and see if you can guess the meaning. If you are not sure of the meaning, ask a classmate or check your dictionary. Once you have found the meanings of all the words and phrases, create your own sentences with the bold-faced words and phrases.

a. Could you please **overnight** the pack to me.

b. I would like you to please **credit my account**.

c. I am going to sue you for **breach of contract**.

d. I would like to exchange it for a product of **equivalent value**.

e. Enclosed are copies of **relevant documents**.

f. I **leased** a brand new sports car.

g. I was **billed** an incorrect amount.

h. The product is still well within its **warranty period**.

i. The person that answered the phone was very **sarcastic**.

a. ______________________________

b. ______________________________

c. ______________________________

d. ______________________________

e. ______________________________

f. ______________________________

g. ______________________________

h. ______________________________

i. ______________________________

LESSON 6 EXAMPLE

Brandon Lee
English House
171 Lay Hung Road
Kowloon, Hong Kong 765
Phone: (212)-997-0034
Cell: (111)-321-7430

September 1, 2011

Janet Fuller
Sales Manager
Super English Books
123 Brooks Ave.
Palm Beach, FL 82331 USA

Dear Ms. Fuller:

Re. Order No. 768197

I am writing to inform you that the books I ordered on Monday August 23rd, order number 768197 from sales representative Chris Nelly at your company did not arrive as ordered.

On Monday August 23rd, I placed an order for twenty *Super English Grammar* books, thirty *Writing Flow* books, and fifty *Eye to Eye* conversation books. However, when the books arrived at our school, we were unable to find the *Super English Grammar* books in any of the boxes. The *Super English Grammar* books, however, were written on the attached receipt showing that we were in fact billed for them. As a result our school had to delay classes for a week, causing us to lose $500.00.

This error put our firm in a difficult position. I would like your company to please send the *Super English Grammar* books immediately. In addition, I would like your company to compensate or school for the money we lost.

I look forward to seeing this problem resolved quickly. I would like you to contact me no later than tomorrow at (212)-997-0034. I would also like the books and our money refunded by this Friday. How this problem is resolved will determine our business relations in the future.

Sincerely,

Brandon Lee

Brandon Lee

enc. Sales receipt from order no. 768197

Assignment

Using the example from page 178 you have to create a complaint letter based on the choices given on the next page. Furthermore, your complaint letter must be placed inside of a correctly addressed envelope. You will be graded according to the chart below. In addition there should be no spelling mistakes. All spelling mistakes will result in an automatic 5 point deduction from your grade.

Followed the correct layout	/5
Wrote a well written complaint letter in accordance with pgs. 170-175	/5
Wrote a well addressed envelope in accordance with pg. 176	/5
Used in, at, and on correctly throughout your letter	/5
Made polite requests using would you and could you	/5
Wrote a realistic complaint and solution	/5
Total Score	/30

Assignment Questions

1. Choose one letter below to write a complaint letter for.

a. You booked a flight with an airline company, however, when you arrived at the airport there were no seats left on the plane.

b. You ordered a cell-phone on-line, however, when it arrived two buttons on the key pad didn't work.

c. You went to a restaurant and in your food there was a piece of plastic that cut your mouth open, requiring you to go to the hospital and get stitches.

d. You bought a new pair of shoes and after just two days the heel broke off.

Assignment Layout

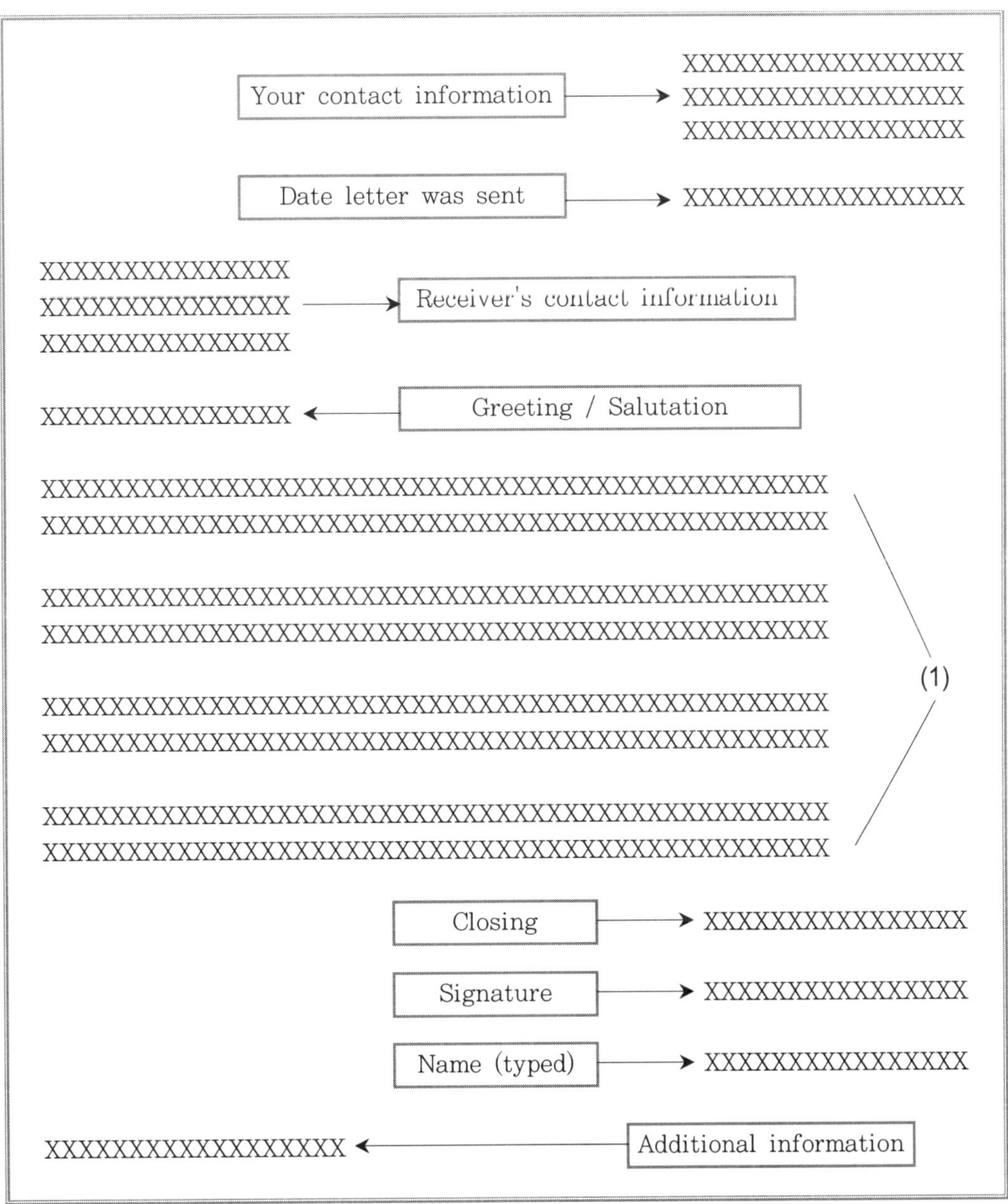

1. Your paragraphs should align evenly on both sides. In addition, your paragraphs should follow the layout detailed on pages 170-175.

Self-Check List

1. Use the check-list below to make sure you have completed the assignment correctly.

Did you...	Yes	No
follow the correct layout?		
write a well written complaint letter in accordance with pgs. 170–175?		
write a well addressed envelope in accordance with pg. 176?		
use in, at, and on correctly throughout your letter?		
make polite requests using would you and could you?		
write a realistic complaint and solution?		
make any spelling mistakes?		

Peer Review

1. Read your partner's complaint letter. Write the name of the place your partner is complaining to. Next, write the reason why they are complaining.

2. Read your partner's complaint letter. Write the solution that your partner is requesting in their letter.

3. Read your partner's complaint letter. When can or would your partner like to be contacted.

4. Use the check-list below to make sure your partner has completed the assignment correctly.

Did your partner...	Yes	No
follow the correct layout?		
write a well written complaint letter in accordance with pgs. 170–175?		
write a well addressed envelope in accordance with pg. 176?		
use in, at, and on correctly throughout your letter?		
make polite requests using would you and could you?		
write a realistic complaint and solution?		
make any spelling mistakes?		

5. Discuss your findings and results with your partner.

Writing Flow

2010년 3월 5일 인쇄
2010년 3월 10일 발행

저 자 ◎ Chad Billiris
발행자 ◎ 조 승 식
발행처 ◎ (주) 도서출판 북 스 힐
서울시 강북구 라일락길 36

등 록 ◎ 제 22-457 호

(02) 994-0071(代)

(02) 994-0073

bookswin@unitel.co.kr
www.bookshill.com

값 12,000 원

ISBN 978-89-5526-668-9